THE BIG FOUR IN COLOUR 1935-50

by

DAVID JENKINSON

In collaboration with

JOHN EDGINGTON *and* JOHN SMART

*I*n the crisp light of a late winter sun, GWR Collett 48xx 0-4-2T No.4837 takes water at Marlow in February 1946. These attractive little engines, introduced in 1932, were the archetypal Great Western branch line motive power in its later years. Fitted for push and pull (auto train) working, they were renumbered later in 1946 into the 14xx series, the 48xx number series being required at the time for 2-8-0 tender engines fitted for oil burning. It is highly probable that most readers who remember the auto-fitted 0-4-2Ts will know them best with their later numbers. The class totalled 75 engines, built between 1932 and 1936 and another 20 examples appeared in 1933, identical in all respects save for their lack of auto gear and numbered 5800-19 so as to differentiate them from the push-pull version. When this picture was taken, the 1939-45 war was only just over and evidence of this is given by the utility 'all-brown' livery of the coach just in shot at the left hand side.

(H.N.James - Ref: GW35)

THE BIG FOUR IN COLOUR 1935-50

By DAVID JENKINSON

In collaboration with JOHN EDGINGTON *and* JOHN SMART

King's Cross 1937 and Gresley Class A1 4-6-2 No.2557 Blair Athol *makes a fine sight getting under way with an unidentified down express.* Blair Athol *was one of the earlier Gresley pacifics (built in 1925) and when this picture was taken, showed little change from the form in which it entered service, including round dome cover and GNR type tender. By 1928, the original Gresley 4-6-2 design had been developed into the familiar A3 type with higher boiler pressure (increased from 180psi to 220psi) and other changes, a condition to which the earlier A1s were eventually converted (mostly during 1939-48 with a few earlier examples), save for one exception, the pioneer A1 No.4470* Great Northern, *which was rebuilt in more drastic form by Edward Thompson in 1945. No.2557 was rebuilt to A3 late in 1945 and later became LNER No.58 (BR 60058). During its BR life (in 1955) it received a replacement LNER standard tender.*

(E.Brightman - Ref: NE105)

TRANSPORT

Atlantic

PUBLISHERS

PENDRAGON
BOOKS

During the 1930s, the railways were in the middle of an economy drive which had started in the 1920s. One option was to reduce the amount of painted decoration on stock and this led to increasing numbers of black engines, less decorative carriage liveries and, in 1936, a decision to abandon the familar large lettering on company owned wagons. For this reason, we imagine, early colour photographers often ignored the black engines and goods trains. But occasionally, things could be untypically colourful, as shown in this undated view at Brookman's Park of an up express freight hauled by LNER Class K3 2-6-0 No.207. The leading wagons all carry the new style livery and two of them are clearly brand new, so the date must be (at the earliest) 1937 and is probably a little later.
(Philip Colebourn Collection)

© *David Jenkinson, Atlantic Transport Publishers and contributors as credited*

Published by
Atlantic Transport Publishers
Trevithick House, West End, Penryn, Cornwall, TR10 8HE. All rights reserved

LAYOUT, DESIGN AND REPRODUCTION Barnabus Design & Print, Truro, Cornwall

PRINTED BY: The Amadeus Press Ltd, Huddersfield, West Yorkshire

British Cataloguing in Publication Data:
A catalogue record for this book is held by the British Library - ISBN 0 906899 62 1

NOTES

1. Many images in this work are also available in 35mm slide form via Messrs Colour-Rail, 5 Treacher's Close, Chesham, Bucks, HP5 2HD, to whom all enquiries should be addressed regarding prices &c. In all cases where copy slides were available at the time of going to press, the caption credit includes the Colour-Rail reference number, which should always be used in any correspondence.

2. All photographs appearing in this book are subject to strict copyright and may not be reproduced in any other publication without prior written permission from the publisher and/or copyright holder. All enquiries should be addressed in the first instance to the publisher.

CONTENTS

*D*ifficult to classify by company but of great interest and rarity, this view shows USA 2-8-0 No.1712 shunting freight at Bishops Stortford (LNER) in 1943. These typically North American locomotives were brought over from the USA to serve duty with the military in Europe, but for a short period prior to the June 1944 invasion of Normandy, they were widely used in Britain, especially (but not exclusively) on the LNER system. At this time in our history, the 2-8-0 was particularly favoured for heavy freight in connection with the requirements of the armed services both at home and overseas and it is significant to recall that our own War Department (WD) was responsible for building many hundreds of 2-8-0s. The first to appear were to the Stanier LMS Class 8F design but they were followed by the much more basic 'WD' type 2-8-0, designed by R.A.Riddles (one time assistant to William Stanier on the LMS). In due course, most of the British-built 2-8-0s came back 'home' to see much valuable service until the very last days of steam; but the American engines never returned, save for a number of latter day re-imports for preservation.
(Philip Colebourn Collection)

Introduction

The idea for this book was formed some years ago, when I first began to realise that an astonishing number of colour transparency images of our railways had survived from the pre-1950 era. Not all of them were very good in quality terms and some of them gave no hope of ever being able to be reproduced in print, but almost all were of great historical interest. But were there enough to justify a full length book? The general concensus was 'probably not' until by great good fortune, two or three hitherto unknown collections (totalling over 100 images) came to my attention by way of photograph submissions for the house magazines which my firm publishes. We were able to negotiate terms (including complete purchase of the largest collection) and the availability of these images, added to those already available via other sources, made this book possible.

None of it could have happened without the active co-operation of Colour-Rail, a firm masterminded by Ron White who, as well as trying to make an 'honest crust' has probably done more than anyone else I know to ensure the survival of these important historical images in a more permanent form than would have been possible had they been simply left 'as taken'. And here, I think it important that a few words should be said about the technical problems involved in making them suitable for printing.

Firstly, of course, no reader should expect quite the same photographic quality as can now be achieved with modern cameras and colour film; but what is amazing is how often, in spite of all difficulties, a truly remarkable result was obtained, for what should be remembered above all is that most pictures in this book date from the days when colour photography was in its infancy. At that time, the most common film available was known as Dufaycolour - it worked at a speed of about 2ASA by the way! This film was temperamental and involved a great deal of individual processing skill, but if properly handled, it could and did give a very beautiful image, often of almost 'oil painting' quality.

The problem is, however, that the original Dufaycolour transparency cannot be 'scanned' for reproduction in the manner of modern slide material. This arises from the nature of the film itself, the image being formed by way of a resau - a series of tiny 'dots' in the three primary colours rather in the manner of the image on a colour television screen. When projected they blend to form a full colour image (again as with TV) and the dots cannot normally be seen with the naked eye. But to make them suitable for printing, they have first to be copied onto a film which can be scanned. By good fortune, this copying (if it can be done before the original has degraded too much) also gives a permanence to the image which the original never had.

Colour-Rail have made a speciality of this sort of operation and I was pleased to entrust them with the copying of the originals which came my way too. As a result, I and my editorial colleagues were eventually able to select from some 500 images for this book, mostly via Colour-Rail and ourselves but not forgetting another small but very valuable collection of copy slides from Philip Colebourn. It is inevitable that a number of the images we have chosen will be quite well known in consequence - some of the pictures have been around for a long time. But they are far too historically important to omit from a work of this nature and we have tried to present them in a properly integrated way, probably for the first time - and there are a lot of completely new ones too!

A word too must also be included on the controversial question of colour accuracy. No

In some cases, the only way to 'rescue' a contemporary colour image is to 'freeze' a single frame from a 16mm cine film source. This is one such example: the experimental LMS three-car articulated diesel unit arriving at Bletchley from Oxford in 1938. Clearly, some definition is lacking, but its rarity value in giving the scarlet and cream livery detail of this short-lived venture surely justifies the effort which was involved in obtaining the copy. For the record, the roof was silver. The unit was one of several pre-war attempts to economise on cross-country and other routes of which the contemporary GWR railcars (featured elsewhere in this book) are perhaps the best known. The LMS unit, though much nearer in interior design concept to the eventual BR multiple unit of the 1950s, had a less useful future than its GWR contemporaries, ending its days as a cut down two-coach service unit - with flattened roof! - for use on the electrified Manchester-Altrincham line.
(The late R.H.R.Garraway - Ref: LM53)

colour image (even the most modern) can be 100% accurate in terms of rendering 'paint on metal or wood', partly because the surface texture of both film and paper is different but also because the eye makes subjective allowances which the camera lens cannot do. The amazing thing is how close the image can often be and Dufay was especially good in this particular respect. We have therefore tried to select views which, with a few exceptions (chosen for their rarity), show the original liveries in an acceptable part of the colour spectrum - their value for checking obscure detail is, of course, self evident.

In addition to this aspect of the subject, we have deliberately sought to achieve a proportionate numerical balance between the Big Four companies, but this in itself was not easy; some companies were better covered than others. We also realised from an early stage that some of the most interesting survivals came from that fascinating transition period (1948-50) before BR standard liveries became common, and we felt that this too had to be covered. In some few cases, the actual pictures were taken after 1950 but our criterion has been that the style represented should have appeared before the end of that year and that only company-designed 'hardware' should feature. And we start in 1935 for no more significant reason than that this is the earliest attributable date on any of the images selected. We also decided to offer a few vintage London Transport locomotives as well since the steam element of this system was very closely linked to the LNER and in 1937, the three classes of larger and more modern locomotives were actually sold to the LNER. For this reason, we have put the LT views in the form of a short 'interlude' after the LNER chapter.

Within each company, the choice was determined mainly by a wish to offer as much variety as possible consistent with quality, particularly in terms of livery and decor, but not forgetting the background detail wherever possible. Most of the pictures, understandably, feature locomotives, but since they were not taken in any systematic way, there is an inevitable lack of total balance. For instance, passenger types tend to dominate (perhaps because they were seen as more 'colourful' subjects at the time) and many highly interesting classes clearly 'escaped' the early colour photographers altogether. But given these caveats, it is surprising how good a cross-section was available and we have chosen to present each chapter along broadly similar lines, with principal passenger types at the top of the list and working 'downwards', so to speak.

Each chapter starts with a brief resumé of the company/theme concerned. It is not our intention that this should be seen as a 'history' in the generally accepted sense, for we appreciate that many readers will have a good grounding in much of the story already; but it did seem helpful, especially for those who are coming 'new' to the historical railway scene, to set out a brief outline at the head of each chapter, if only to avoid unnecessary repetition of detail in the captions themselves.

While on this latter subject, I felt that since, barring a miraculous (and large!) new 'find', this exercise is unlikely ever to be repeated, it was rather important to make sure (as best I could) that the accompanying caption detail was as comprehensive as possible; these images, no matter how randomly taken they may have been, are the real stuff of railway history and deserve nothing less. So, working on the basis that two heads are better than one, and three even better still, I asked two of my good friends, John Edgington and John Smart if they would like to get involved. Both of them combine a deep knowledge of railway history with considerable experience in the handling and

This view is one of the older pictures to have survived - M&GNR 0-6-0 No.89 in M&GNR livery at Edmondthorpe, 1936 - and although the colour is restrained, its presence does give a good impression of the general state of affairs at the time - not very good, if truth be told! In October 1936, after a long period of supervision by the Midland/LMS companies, the old Midland and Great Northern engines were taken into LNER stock and quickly renumbered by the new owners, if not scrapped! Most M&GN locomotives were either 'home' built or of Derby (MR) origin but No.89 was one of a batch of twelve, built in 1900 by Dubs & Co. to an Ivatt design identical to those provided for one of the two parent companies: GNR Class J4 (later LNER Class J3). They carried M&GN numbers 81-92 and from c.1933, Deeley pattern smokeboxes and doors began to be fitted (reflecting the continuing Midland influence) and this resulted in some strange and not entirely beneficial changes to their appearance. For one thing, the smokebox door centres were often set below the boiler centre line with curious aesthetic results as seen here. No.89 became LNER No.089 in April 1937 and LNER No.4164 under the 1946 numbering scheme; it was scrapped in 1947. (H.N.James - Ref: NE37)

classifying of photographic images and we have spent many happy hours both putting this set of views together and debating what should be said about them - I am greatly indebted to them both. Nor must I omit to acknowledge my grateful thanks to Ron White for his own valuable contribution in advising on locations and dates (not to mention suitability for reproduction) and also for making available the best copies possible from which to prepare the book.

Last but not least, I would like to think that this book serves as modest tribute to those pioneering photographers who were prepared to experiment with colour film in its infancy at a time when our railways were passing through one of the most interesting periods of their history. Many of these photographers are known by name (happily a number of them are still with us) and their names given with the captions where this is the case; but other names have been 'lost in the mists of time', more's the pity.

Overall, therefore, the assembly of this book has been very much a 'team operation' from the outset. Our aim has been to use the whole available range of these unique images in order to present as comprehensive a colour overview of our traditional railway system as is possible for the last 15 years or so of its pre-corporate appearance. We have tried to do it in a way that has never been attempted before; and if you the reader gain half as much pleasure from perusing it as we have from putting it together, we shall be well pleased.

April 1994

These views, taken at Brighton Works simultaneously in 1946, should serve to illustrate the problems faced by the early users of colour film and reinforce the textual comments regarding colour accuracy. The first is from Dufaycolour, the second from the then 'new' Kodachrome film - still very slow speed (8 ASA) but much easier to use than Dufay. There are two interesting points at issue: the exact shade of green on the newly painted tender of the unidentified Bulleid 4-6-2, known to be malachite, and the real colour of the 'yellow' 0-6-0T. Kodachrome clearly reproduces the green colour rather darker than in reality and the Dufay is thus more accurate for this well known shade. The problem is more difficult in the case of the works shunter, Stroudley Class A1X 0-6-0T, now No.377s and decked out in the full finery of original 'Improved Engine Green' livery with tanks lettered in traditional fashion. At this time, it may be presumed that Brighton had better evidence of the London Brighton and South Coast livery than in more modern days and in the absence of contemporary colour views of LB&SCR engines, this engine is about as definitive a historical source as one is likely to get. But which of the two reproduced shades is the nearer? On the whole, the Dufay seems better since it conveys the 'mustard' overtone which the Kodachrome lacks. If so, the historical value of all Dufays in this survey is self-evident, regardless of technical problems.
J.M.Jarvis - Ref: SR17)

LONDON MIDLAND AND SCOTTISH RAILWAY

It would be quite inappropriate to start the LMS chapter of this book with any other subject than a red engine to LMS standard design hauling a train of LMS standard stock, for this image represented perhaps the most obviously different aspect of the company compared with its contemporaries. The livery colour (which was inherited from the Midland) was unique amongst the Big Four and the railway pursued standardisation 'across the board' to a much greater extent than did the other three.

But this picture is not as typical as it might seem, not least because it was actually taken in 1949 and not on LMS metals at all; and although the train is bound for the LMS route to Bristol, the location is Holgate Bridge, York, very much part of former LNER (ex-NER) territory. Furthermore, although the view shows no sign of corporate BR ownership at all, it was exceedingly rare to see a red engine at all after the war, the LMS having standardised black for the whole of its fleet in 1946 (with a bit of red lining for the express types).

The explanation is that after the war, the LMS conducted livery experiments in 1946 prior to making a final decision and repainted just one locomotive in the old colours to compare it with other possible schemes. It is this unique engine, Stanier Class 5XP 4-6-0 No.5594 Bhopal, which is seen here. The lettering is of a new sans serif type (which was adopted), but there is little lining compared with pre-war days, and none at all on either splasher or tender sides. However, the livery itself looks in generally good state, given that it had been applied three years previously and routine maintenance was still difficult. As far as can be seen, the train itself consists wholly of standard Stanier LMS stock built to designs of which the first were introduced in 1932 and multiplied thereafter in huge quantities. (E. Sanderson - Ref: LM81)

An Introduction to the LMS

The LMS was by far the largest of the Big Four railways created by the 1923 Grouping and was also the most difficult to integrate into a coherent whole. This was largely because contained within the newly unified system were two hitherto rival English companies, the London & North Western and Midland Railways, not to mention their respective Scottish allies, the Caledonian and Glasgow & South Western. If to this highly combustible mixture one then adds the many other proud companies which were also incorporated in the LMS, it will readily be appreciated what a difficult task was faced by its first managers. Sadly, however, traditional rivalries took a long time to settle down and the LMS did not really 'get its act together' (to use modern idiom) until the early 1930s, just before the start of the period covered by this book. All that needs to be added is that for those who wish to know more of this fascinating story, there is ample literature currently available.

Geographically, the LMS system was by far the most comprehensive of any of the Big Four. It stretched from the far north of Scotland to the south coast of England (the latter via shared interests), from west to east coasts in both Scotland and England and had a virtual monopoly of North Wales, thanks to the LNWR. Collectively it embraced no fewer than eight main pre-Group constituents, plus a few 'bits and pieces' as well, not to mention significant interests in Ireland via both the LNWR and particularly the MR in Ulster. Unfortunately, these Irish areas of influence have not generated any early colour images and cannot, therefore, be included in this book.

The LMS system included three out of the five major pre-1923 companies in Scotland. Two, the CR and G&SWR, have already been mentioned which between them just about wrapped up the western half of the Southern Uplands and Central Lowlands of Scotland - and a fair amount of the 'middle ground' too, not to mention penetrating branches into rival territory. The Caledonian went as far north as Ballachulish on the west coast and Aberdeen on the east, while linked to it at Perth, and covering most of the area north thereof, save for a small enclave occupied by the Great North of Scotland Railway, which went to the LNER, ran the tentacles of the Highland Railway, the third Scottish constituent of the LMS - a fascinating company which controlled all railways north of Inverness.

In England, the already mentioned LNWR and MR controlled two of the three Anglo-Scottish routes south of the border, one via the West Midlands and Crewe (LNWR) the other via the East Midlands and Derby (MR). These routes converged only in Carlisle, where they shared the same joint station and in London itself, half a mile apart along the Euston Road at Euston and St Pancras. But between these two points, they were in constant rivalry in many areas, far too numerous to mention here. In the industrial heartland of the north of England, both of them were also intricately intermixed with the lines of the Lancashire and Yorkshire Railway, an accurately named company which had amalgamated with the LNWR a year before the main grouping and which gave the LMS access to the East Coast of England via the former LYR facility at Goole.

In the Lake District, the area to the west of the LNWR main line over Shap Fell was largely the fiefdom of the Maryport and Carlisle and Furness Railways. Between them, they had numerous arrangements with the much larger LNWR and MR companies but they remained small, fiercely independent concerns. Finally, in terms of main constituents, the LMS was completed by the North Staffordshire Railway, centred around Stoke-on-Trent. This relatively small company, like the larger LYR, was also aptly named and, again like the LYR, was closely linked with territory of interest to the LNWR and MR - this time in the Crewe-Derby area. The LMS also absorbed other small concerns (eg the Wirral and the Knott End Railways) and had a stake in numerous joint operations, principal amongst which were the Somerset and Dorset (with the SR), by which it gained access to the south coast, and the Midland and Great Northern (with the LNER) which took it to the East Anglian coast, its second East Coast outlet in England.

More than any other of the Big Four, the LMS pursued standardisation, in which respect it eventually outstripped the GWR in quantitative terms (Chapter 4). Thus, by the time the pictures in this book were taken, much of the 1923 variety, if it had not vanished completely, was quite rare and the picture selection inevitably reflects this fact. Furthermore, although the LMS adopted Midland colours for its livery, giving it an element of uniqueness by contrast with the others, the fact is that in terms of early colour photography, it does not, in proportion to its size, seem to have attracted quite as much interest as the other three. In view of its early espousal of black for most engines (save for a handful of more modern types), this is maybe not too surprising; even so, a good cross-section of images has survived, albeit somewhat biassed in favour of the more glamorous engines.

In 1923, the LMS re-numbered all its inherited engines in systematic new blocks by company and class, save for those of the MR which retained their pre-group numbers; and new engines were allocated vacant blocks of sequential numbers. Other numbering detail, where relevant, is given with the captions.

OPPOSITE, BELOW: *In the late 1930s, streamlining was all the rage and the LMS contribution was a developed version of the Stanier pacific, the 'Coronation' Class. These engines had numerous technical improvements, along with an increase in driving wheel size from the 6ft 6in of the 'Princesses' to 6ft 9in. But the most noticeable feature was the streamlined casing and a new blue livery. When the engines were being run-in from Crewe (both when new and after overhaul) it was customary to send them to Shrewsbury on trial before releasing them back to traffic and this view was taken there in 1938 on just such an occasion. It shows the last of the five examples built in 1937, No.6224 Princess Alexandra, confusingly, in view of the earlier 4-6-2s, one of two examples of the later design to bear a 'Princess' name. The 'streamlined' lamps are worthy of note, also the degree to which the locomotive displays weathering around the casing joints. Note too that the cab roof is coloured below the rainstrip - the normal pre-war LMS practice for this class, streamlined or otherwise. In later years, with the class all in the non-streamlined form, the BR custom was to paint the whole roof black. (The late P.B. Whitehouse - Ref: LM20)*

What better way to start this survey than with the only known pre-war colour picture of the record breaking Stanier 4-6-2 No.6201 Princess Elizabeth *herself? This engine, along with sister locomotive, No.6200* The Princess Royal, *introduced the pacific wheel arrangement to the LMS in 1933, a year after their designer, William Stanier, had come to the LMS from the GWR. They were not, at first, wholly successful and a third boiler (with higher superheat) had to be made before they began to 'perform'. This allowed the first two boilers, successively, to be modified and the situation was transformed. In 1936, with the new (domed) boiler,* Princess Elizabeth *was tested non-stop between London and Glasgow (and return), putting up record sub-6hr performances in both directions, thus paving the way for the later 4-6-2 design, the streamlined 'Coronation' Class - see next views. In this picture,* Princess Elizabeth *was photographed at Crewe in August 1938, recently outshopped with one of the two original domeless boilers, now modified with higher superheat.* (L.Hanson - Ref: LM30)

The streamlined 4-6-2s were designed to run the 'Coronation Scot' express, like its LNER 'Coronation' equivalent (see Chapter 2), a suitably patriotic gesture in 1937. By strange coincidence, both companies chose blue liveries, rather than retain their usual colour schemes; and the LMS copied its shade from that of the pre-1923 Caledonian Railway. The decorative embellishment was silver, edged dark blue (the wheels were also dark blue and the nameplates chrome plated with a dark blue background) and this view of No.6222 Queen Mary *leaving Euston with the down 'Coronation Scot' in June 1938, gives an amazingly accurate rendition of the colour, once again a tribute to the fidelity of the original Dufaycolour (see Introduction), in no way impaired by the evidence of slight movement 'blur'.* (The late H.L.Overend - Ref: LM65)

OPPOSITE, BELOW: *For many years, the previous view (and another one taken with it) were thought to be the only colour views of the red LMS streamliners. But in 1993, this one turned up in all its glory, having been submitted to the publisher's office by a gentleman from North America! It shows the last of the 1938 streamliners on show at Flushing (New York Central) on 30th April 1939 where it was on display in connection with the 1939 New York World Fair Exhibition. The LMS had been invited to send its 'Coronation Scot' train to this event and duly obliged in the form of such carriages of its proposed new 1940 train as had been finished (the war prevented completion as planned), along with its newest streamlined engine, which happened to be No.6229* Duchess of Hamilton. *For obvious publicity reasons, the LMS gave it the identity of No.6220* Coronation *and as such it is seen here, complete with American headlamp and bell which it carried while running in the USA. It returned to Britain in 1942 and resumed proper identity; meantime the pioneer No.6220 ran as a blue 6229! In this view, the crimson is seen as a much deeper shade than in the previous picture. This is a direct consequence of the 'fall of light' which makes dark red engines especially difficult to render with accuracy on colour film, a point which will be addressed again with later views in this chapter.* (Courtesy Paul Lubliner, San Diego)

When the LMS built its next batch of streamliners in 1938, a decision was made to revert to the traditional Midland Crimson Lake colour and five new engines emerged in this colour scheme, which many thought to be much richer and more dignified and was, in any case, rather more appropriate when engines were in charge of those trains (all except the 'Coronation Scot' in fact) which carried the usual coaching stock livery. This fact is well brought out in this 'freeze frame' view from a contemporary 16mm cine film which shows No.6227 Duchess of Devonshire leaving Euston in 1938. In spite of the slightly blurred nature of the original film, the gold striping with its vermilion and black edging, is clearly apparent. (J.F.Traxler - Ref: LM50)

It is a fairly well known fact that William Stanier was not at all convinced of the value of streamlining, regarding it as a wasteful extravagance, likely to get in the way of easy maintenance. He agreed to it being applied to his second 4-6-2 design in 1937 solely to satisfy the publicity men, but when the next ten engines were under consideration in 1938, he argued the case that five 'proper ones', as he called them, should be built for comparative purposes! Numbered 6230-4 in sequence after the five red streamliners, these were the original 'Duchesses' of popular perception and time was to prove Stanier right when, after the war, all the shrouded engines were de-steamlined and assumed much the same appearance, albeit with some detail variations, as the original five non-streamliners had first displayed. In this view, No.6232 Duchess of Montrose *displays its fine proportions at Shrewsbury on the return leg of a running-in turn from Crewe in 1938. It was later, like all the class, to receive double chimney and smoke deflectors.* (The late P.B.Whitehouse - Ref: LM21)

As with the red streamliners, the previous view was, for many years, thought to be the only pre-war colour image of that particular type of locomotive - until this one emerged, again by chance, in 1991. It shows No.6232 again, also in 1938 but this time leaving Euston. The original Dufay was very dark and by no means perfect, but it clearly showed the richness of the LMS crimson livery together with the gold insignia specially used on this group of five engines. On close examination (though not entirely revealed in the copy) one can also distinguish the gold lining (with vermilion edging) which was applied to Nos.6230-4, rather than the customary yellow lining. The fireman is looking back for the guard's signal and the chosen angle of view clearly emphasises the massive proportions of these engines, the largest of any British 4-6-2s. (The late Sydney Perrier, courtesy C.S.Perrier - Ref: LM74)

Prior to the arrival of the 4-6-2s, the 'Royal Scots' were the principal express engines on the LMS, but since the pacifics were only few in number, especially prior to the war, the Scots remained at the forefront of activity. Rebuilding with taper boilers (at Stanier's behest) started in 1943, but during the 'red' period, the original parallel boiler form reigned supreme, save for one taper boilered prototype, No.6170, dating from 1935 - not illustrated here. This very early (April 1937) picture at Crewe Works shows No.6149 The Middlesex Regiment *(the last of the original 50 engines, dating from 1927 and named* Lady of the Lake *until 1936), newly outshopped with replacement Stanier tender. It is also of interest in displaying the slight changes in LMS red livery which were first introduced in 1937 and which were particularly well 'caught' by the early colour film, almost to the point of domination. These were the brighter chrome yellow lines (replacing the previous 'straw' shade) and the bright yellow insignia, with equally bright vermilion shading.* (The late J.P.Mullett - Ref: LM46)

This late evening view, taken at Crewe North in May 1939, shows No.6100 Royal Scot *itself, displaying all the variations in the parallel boiler form which had been incorporated prior to general rebuilding of the class with taper boilers. Most noticeable are the larger Stanier tender (acquired by exchange with those originally attached to new 'Jubilee' 4-6-0s - see later) and the final 'curved top' smoke deflectors. Once again the new 1937 style lining and insignia are very clearly represented but the numeral size is only 12in, very common for many LMS express engines of the time but not as widely seen on the Scots as the 14in variety shown in the previous view.*

This engine was not the original Royal Scot, *the latter having exchanged identity permanently with the then fairly new No.6152 in connection with a trip to the USA in 1933 for the Century of Progress exhibition. The engine carried a welter of Stanier modifications for this event (many of them later applied to the whole class) and unlike the later 'excursion' of No.6229 - above - the LMS decided that since this was the actual engine which had been to North America, it should remain thus identified - ie by way of commemorative additions to the nameplate and an American style bell, the latter just visible in the shadow between the smoke deflectors.* (W.Potter - Ref: LM31)

The Royal Scots having successfully taken over the heaviest workings from 1928, the LMS soon turned to the intermediate express workings. These were usually in the hands of LYR design 4-6-0s, Midland/LMS compound 4-4-0s (both considered later) and four cylinder LNWR 'Claughtons' (not illustrated); but something more modern was felt to be needed. Some of the Claughtons had been fitted with new and larger boilers from 1928, to their considerable advantage, and once the Scots had proved their worth, it was not long before the LMS decided to 'marry' this new boiler to the three-cylinder 'Scot type' chassis. The result was the ever popular 'Patriot' Class which, like the large boilered Claughtons were put in a new 5XP power category to denote their superiority over the existing 5P engines; the Scots were, of course, 6P and the pacifics (which came later), 7P. In this view, Patriot No.5537 Private E.Sykes, V.C. is seen on characteristic duty in 1938 climbing out of Kendal with a Windermere-Manchester train. The engine is red(!), and one can see some sheen beneath the grime, but the LMS worked its express power intensively at that time and the grubby state was not entirely untypical, though not usually as bad as this!
(The late A.E.R.Cope - Ref: LM17)

The new 5XPs were officially called 'Patriots' (using the name given to the first of them as a class designation), but this was mainly because enginemen had quickly dubbed them 'Baby Scots' when they first appeared, a nickname which was frowned on by officialdom. They were regarded as Claughton replacements (not rebuilds) and until 1934, carried the same running numbers as the replaced engines. Some official documents even called them three-cylinder Claughtons; but this picture shows how apt was the informal designation given by the crews. They were indeed, 'miniature' Scots and very fine engines too. This attractive portrait was taken at Edge Hill in June 1939 and shows No.5531 Sir Frederick Harrison with a full tender of coal about to go off on duty. The aforementioned changes to the lining and insignia from 1937 are again prominent and this time, the engine is pretty clean - a more typical state. All told, 52 Patriots were built and eighteen of them were subsequently rebuilt with taper boilers to Class 6P just after the war, becoming fully interchangeable with the Royal Scots in terms of work capability. In this guise, they are featured again in Chapter 6. (W.Potter - Ref: LM36)

When Stanier arrived on the LMS in 1932, the Patriots were already doing some fine work and the 5XP concept clearly suited LMS management; in fact, Stanier authorised the building of further Patriots pending the introduction of his own taper boilered version. These new engines appeared in 1934 and were all unnamed at first. It was not until 1935, when one of them was given black livery with chrome embellishments and named Silver Jubilee, that naming commenced. In due course, this led to the whole class been known as 'Jubilees'. Eventually, 191 of them were built, more than the sum total of pacifics, Scots and Patriots, and a remarkably good cross section of early colour views of this most typical of all the LMS six-coupled express engines has survived. This first one is the earliest to be found and shows No.5647 Sturdee leaving Rugby on a parcels train in 1936 with a 'Horwich' 2-6-0 No.2935 shunting in the left middle distance. The engine is domeless, which was the original state of the first 113 examples (Nos.5552-664). Over the years there were to be many changes. (Colour-Rail - Ref: LM16)

The Jubilees were not quite right at first and early experiments revealed the need for more superheat and altered draughting. This led, in turn, to a decision to build the final examples with a new type boiler, incorporating these changes and also having a longer firebox and a genuine dome. The top feed (which on the first 113 examples looked like a dome) was now covered by a smaller casing in front of the dome proper. These features are all seen on this view of No.5677 Beatty at Crewe North shed in August 1938, the longer firebox being identified at this angle of view by virtue of the small dome-shaped cover plates to the wash-out apertures on the shoulder of the firebox. This picture is also of interest in showing the pre-1937 form of pale yellow (straw) lining with gold leaf insignia and black shading. All told, 78 Jubilees were built new to this configuration (Nos.5665-742), (L.Hanson - Ref: LM35)

ABOVE: *Over the years, the Jubilees ran with a variety of tenders, though most of them were coupled to the familiar Stanier curved top type when new. But many of them lost their 4000 gallon tenders in exchange for Fowler 3500 gallon tenders from the 70 Royal Scots c.1936. Others were given Stanier 3500 gallon tenders (these are very difficult to tell apart from the 4000 gallon type in many pictures, see next view); while ten of them were paired with a very ugly flat sided tender, intermediate in design between the Fowler and Stanier standard versions. One such is seen here attached to No.5616* Malta *at St Albans in 1938. This engine was built with domeless boiler but has now been given a domed version of this type. It also sports the 1937 style of lining and insignia. The train is not identified but is likely to have been the 'Thames-Clyde Express', the leading vehicle being one of the rare 1927 brake firsts which were rostered at the head of this train for many years.*

(Philip Colebourn Collection)

OPPOSITE, BELOW: *A gleaming No.5694* Bellerophon *stands in Shrewsbury, almost certainly running-in from Crewe Works, in 1938. The engine is one of the later long firebox variants and although partly obscured by the canopies, the tender is identified as a 4000 gallon example by the positioning of the very pronounced row of rivets above the 'LMS' - see previous view. Comparison of this picture with the previous one reveals a very different rendition of the Crimson Lake colour, though the chrome yellow lining and insignia stand out clearly in both cases. Observation of real-life examples of red engines in preservation makes it clear that this rich shade can vary in its apparent hue from a bright, almost 'pillar box' red to a deep maroon, sometimes even with a hint of purple. This variation is almost always determined by the angle of sunlight in relation to the observer's eye, or even the lack of sunshine altogether. In most cases, the observer will then make a subconscious mental adjustment to the light and 'see' the correct shade; but the camera cannot do this!* (The late P.B.Whitehouse - Ref: LM55)

18

This sparkling view shows one of the most famous of all the Jubilees, No.5660 Rooke *at Crewe North in August 1938. It was a Leeds based engine at the time and may be off-works after overhaul; the state of the livery would certainly support this supposition. Once again, lining and insignia are the brighter 1937 style and the engine trails a Stanier 3500 gallon tender. These had a shorter wheelbase than the 4000 gallon type (not always apparent at casual glance) and could best be distinguished by the fact that the first horizontal row of rivets above the 'LMS' was set further below the top edge of the rearward extension of the side panels behind the coal space than on the 4000 gallon type.* Rooke *was famous for its record breaking test runs between Bristol, Leeds and Carlisle (and return) in 1937 which confirmed that all the original teething troubles with these engines had been cured. It is seen here with the domed version of the original boiler, reflecting the fact that from 1936 onwards, all domeless Jubilees had been converted to domed form.* (L.Hanson - Ref: LM34)

ABOVE: *The review of Jubilees is concluded with a picture of No.5601* British Guiana *on a down express at Birmingham New Street which might, perhaps, have been more appropriate to Chapter 6, for it was taken on 6th July 1948. But it has been put here because it is the only known contemporary colour view of the official 1946 LMS express passenger locomotive livery - gloss black with maroon (not called crimson lake now, be it noted!) and straw insignia. As can be seen, when kept clean it could look very smart but it does rather lend support to the view that the LMS was not regarded by photographers as being too colourful during the later 1940s. The engine is coupled (somewhat less commonly for a Jubilee) to a 4000 gallon tender with flush welded side panels and the leading coach is in BR experimental 'plum and spilt milk' livery, giving an almost 'LNWR Look' to the whole ensemble; even the location is appropriate!* (E.S.Russell - Ref: LM70)

OPPOSITE, TOP: *Yet another apparent shade of red is offered in this broadside view of No.5691* Orion, *waiting to attach to a train at Crewe station in 1939. Here, the engine is clean, but slightly dusty and the light almost broadside, both of which will have an effect. It is also perhaps worth mentioning that the 1937 style lining and lettering is not as dominant in this view as in some earlier pictures, maybe also because of the light. But we venture to suggest that a rather more natural appearance has resulted in consequence. The angle of view also clearly reveals the distinguishing aspects of the final 78 Jubilees with the longer firebox: the division between firebox and tapered boiler barrel can be seen to be directly above the centre driving axle whereas in the earlier examples, this division was noticeably further back.* (The late P.B.Whitehouse - Ref: LM24)

OPPOSITE, BELOW: *At the introduction to this chapter, a 1949 view was offered of the only LMS engine to be repainted red after the war: Jubilee No.5594* Bhopal; *though, for the record, it is worth stating that a few pre-war red ones also survived to BR. In this view of an up express at Saxby in August 1946, the engine is seen only a few months after repainting; but it must be stated that the red livery does not look as smart as it did three years later! The picture is also of historical value in showing a nice example of the LMS 'Commencement of speed restriction' board and, at the start of the re-laid track, a pair of typical LMS standard upper quadrant signal arms mounted on what looks very much like an original Midland Railway sub-structure.* (H.N.James - Ref: LM47)

OPPOSITE, ABOVE: *Contemporarily with the Jubilees, William Stanier introduced the first of what was eventually to become a very large class of 842 locomotives; the well known Class 5 (originally 5P5F) 4-6-0s. Like so many other work-a-day types, they do not seem to have appealed to the early colour photographers and only two early views have come to light. In this picture, an example of the earliest series, No.5014, is seen at work in one of the first areas of the LMS where these fine engines began to show their mettle: the Highland main line. The location is Slochd Summit (on the 'direct' cut-off line between Aviemore and Inverness via Tomatin) in August 1938 and the train is, typically, an express freight bound for Inverness. The livery would have been lined black (sic!) and by this time, the engine may have acquired the smaller 10in numerals which were common in Scotland after 1936. The engine is dome-less, as were all the original 225 Class 5s, and in later years many received higher superheat and/or domed boilers, just as with the Jubilees. But unlike the domeless Jubilees, all of which eventually received domed boilers, a majority of the original domeless Class 5s remained thus to the end of their lives, albeit with higher superheat and including, it is thought, the example featured here.* (Colour-Rail Ref: LM1)

ABOVE: *Apart from the Midland/LMS compound 4-4-0s, which will be considered later, few pre-war colour pictures survive which show the red livery on earlier designs than those already considered and this is the only one capable of reproduction. It shows 'Lanky Dreadnought' No.10432, one of 70 superheated Class 5P 4-6-0s of Lancashire and Yorkshire design which bore much of the heavier express traffic (along with LNWR Claughtons) before the advent of the three-cylinder 4-6-0s already covered. The engines were built in both LYR and early LMS days, the example shown emerging in December 1922, a few days before the Grouping. There is little sign of red paint on the boiler, though the hint of red suggests that it is there under the filth, given that the cab and tender side panels both reveal the new 1937 style insignia and that paint and lining is in fair condition both there and on the running plate angle and splasher sides. Whatever the reason, it is fair to say that although the LMS was not always the smartest of railways, red engines were not usually as bad as this! No.10432 was seen in 1937, waiting with an express at Ansdell and Fairhaven on the south coast of the Fylde peninsula between Lytham and St Annes. The first coach is a former Midland non-corridor clerestory, express train status notwithstanding; and the location is unusual for any photographer at the time, much less one with colour film!* (The late Edwin Ashworth - Ref: LM75)

OPPOSITE, BELOW: *As with the Jubilees, so too with the Class 5s, all later examples from No.5225 onwards were built from new with domed boilers and longer fireboxes but, as stated, some of the earlier domeless variety were also given domed boilers and this picture shows one such, No.5131 at Crewe North shed in August 1938. The picture is a rare colour example of the short-lived '1936 livery' in which the LMS substituted sans serif insignia for its previous scroll and serif type. The characters remained gold (gilt) as before but the back-shading became bright vermilion instead of the earlier blended red and was applied to most types - hitherto most red engines had been given black shading. A great number of Class 5s received this style with the lined black livery (many repaints and the whole of the new domed 5225-451 series during 1936-7); but it is said that signalmen found these new style numbers difficult to read, especially when trains passed at speed. At all events, later in 1937, the LMS reverted to its older insignia shape, but now offered in bright chrome yellow with bright red shading, again for all types as has been described earlier. In this view, by way of bonus, the 14in version of these new style figures can be seen on the cabside of Royal Scot No.6126 Royal Army Service Corps* ((L.Hanson - Ref: LM37)

Prior to the Grouping, the LNWR was by far the biggest user of 4-6-0s as far as the LMS constituents were concerned and although many former LNWR engines were rapidly scrapped as new standard types came into service, some classes survived very well, most notably the 0-8-0s. Of the LNWR passenger types, the 'Prince of Wales' 4-6-0s were the most numerous and amongst the newest, and they too had a reasonable lifespan. Second only to the Claughtons in terms of their importance on the heaviest LNWR express services, the Princes, with 6ft 3in driving wheels, also did valuable service in the mixed traffic role at the higher end of the speed range (intermediate express passenger, fitted freight &c) and it was only when the Class 5s came into service in quantity and began to establish what was almost an operating monopoly of such work, that the LNWR Princes began to be reduced in significant numbers.

In this very early 1936 view, No.25749 is seen passing St Annes Old Links Halt on just a typical mid-1930s duty: an excursion train travelling at a speed which 1/100th of a second exposure could not 'freeze' even at this distance - but what an interesting picture! The train is a typical LMS 'mixed bag' of pre-group corridor stock of a kind spared from scrapping mainly because of the occasional need to exhume them for such duties: two LYR types followed by two Midland clerestories and what looks like a low-roofed LNWR example, with two LYR or LNWR high roofed coaches at the rear. This is another rare view - see previous image - from the late Mr Ashworth who was clearly active in the South Fylde area at the time. Sadly, only a few images have survived, and only these two in a form which can be reproduced. (The late Edwin Ashworth - Ref: LM68)

OPPOSITE, BELOW:*This second similar view of a Belpaire-boilered Prince was taken at Crewe in August 1938 and shows un-named No.25841 awaiting works attention to a front buffer plank, crumpled in an accident. This was one of the later examples to be built, revealed by the sandbox position above the footplate ahead of the long splasher. The livery detail is as described for No.25683 (above) but the more broadside elevation serves to clarify the exact positioning of the lettering &c. In this context, it is worth recalling that at about the time the surviving old LNWR locomotives went onto the 'duplicate' list in the mid-1930s (by having 20000 added to their original LMS numbers), Crewe Works suddenly began to start applying shaded insignia and red lining to many passenger/mixed traffic engines and did so in the paint shop, whereas hitherto, many had been given plain black livery with handpainted, unshaded characters, applied in the erecting shop. The re-numbering was to allow the old number blocks to be re-used for new standard engines, mainly Stanier 4-6-0s and 2-8-0s in the 5xxx and 8xxx series; but dare one surmise that the increased attention to livery was Crewe's way of indicating that its older products were still quite important?* (L.Hanson - Ref: LM40)

ABOVE: *The '19in Goods' 4-6-0s, so-called because of their cylinder diameter, were an early form of quasi-mixed traffic locomotive on the LNWR. Introduced in 1908, their ranks were decimated after the arrival of the Stanier Class 5s and only two reached the duplicate 2xxxx list (for explanation see above), one of which, No.8824 is seen here at Berkhamsted in 1938, still with its first LMS number which was never, in fact, re-used. The engine, destined to be the last survivor (early 1950), retains its original round topped firebox (many had Belpaires in like manner to the Prince of Wales type) and, again like the Princes, the cab profile is to the revised LMS style. The livery is typically scruffy plain black with hand painted numerals and letters while the working is characteristic of the freight trains (the LMS rarely called them 'goods' trains) seen throughout the system at the time; it is carrying 'Through Freight' headlamps, which meant little more than running more than 15 miles without stopping. Apart from the second vehicle (probably coal) and possibly one or two similar examples further back, all the wagons are sheeted-down 'opens', a far more likely choice for most merchandise in those days than the much rarer covered vans.* (Philip Colebourn Collection).

OPPOSITE, ABOVE: *Although the cab roof never changed once the new shape had been determined by the LMS, the round top/Belpaire boilers were interchangeable and it was not uncommon for any one engine to change style more than once. In this evocative view, taken at Birmingham New Street in 1938, the soon to be quite celebrated No.25673 Lusitania is in charge. It was 'celebrated' for all the wrong reasons however, largely because it was one of the last few survivors with a name. It displays the round top firebox configuration and the livery is a somewhat grimy lined black. It is carrying express headcode but the working is not known and the precise carriage types on the train cannot be determined; but they appear to be LNWR, as are the signals and the non-corridor brake third in the adjacent platform which is from the Bowen Cooke 'toplight' period, painted in simplified LMS livery.* (The late P.B.Whitehouse - Ref: LM27)

OPPOSITE, BELOW: *In this fine study, a fairly newly shopped No.25725 is seen at Shrewsbury in 1938 on a cross-country express. This shows the round top firebox combined with the later sandbox position above the footplate and ahead of the splashers, thus denoting one of the later series of engines. Once again, the livery is a smartly maintained lined black with the 1937 pattern yellow/red insignia. Most of the carriages are of the Stanier style but the leading vehicle is a 52ft 6in seven-compartment corridor third of LNWR origin whose styling places it in the early Bowen Cooke era. It would almost certainly have been added to strengthen the formation. Most of the surrounding infrastructure is still solidly pre-1923 and while not, perhaps, quite such a period piece as the previous view, the picture does show that the essential 'LNWR look' (livery excepted) remained strongly in evidence during the LMS period.* (The late P. B. Whitehouse - Ref: LM39)

Apart from the LNWR and LYR, the only LMS constituents to use 4-6-0s were to be found in Scotland. In the case of the Caledonian and G&SWR, both of which were perhaps better described as '4-4-0 lines', they did not figure prominently and most examples were withdrawn quite early. In consequence, this delightful picture is the only known pre-war colour image of either a CR or G&SWR 4-6-0. It was taken at Oban shed in 1938 and shows Pickersgill 191 Class 4-6-0 (LMS Power class 3P) No.14622 in sparkling lined black livery. These pretty little machines dated from 1922, thus spending most of their time as LMS engines. They were built for the Oban line to replace ageing 4-4-0s - hence the 'lightweight' nature of the design.

The lined black livery (introduced by the LMS as an 'intermediate' style in place of red for older passenger and mixed traffic engines from 1928 onwards) suited this class very well and this picture shows a characteristic 'Scottish' variation. When the LMS re-introduced scroll/serif characters in 1937 (above), the new colour was bright chrome yellow, shaded vermilion; but for some unknown reason, though the fact itself is well authenticated, St Rollox works (ex-CR) seems to have had them supplied in the older gold (gilt) colour, but with the new-style bright red shading - and these gold characters are clearly seen on this engine. The smaller 10in numerals also displayed here were also something of a Scottish speciality at this time for all repaints, whereas in England they were only used if larger figures would not fit the locomotive - and even then they were yellow not gold. (Colour-Rail - Ref: LM3)

The Highland Railway introduced the 4-6-0 to Britain as early as 1894 in the form of the well known Jones Goods of which, unfortunately, no vintage colour views have been found. Unsurprisingly, developments followed in due course and there emerged the first of what is best described as a passenger version of the design, though if truth be told, most HR engines had to display 'mixed traffic' capability and the driving wheel size of most of these new engines was only 5ft 9in (the last three, built in 1917 had 6ft wheels). The 'Castles', as they were called, were introduced in 1900 and attributed to Peter Drummond but were, in all essentials, David Jones' last design, details having been worked out before his retirement. Drummond made a few, mostly cosmetic changes (including the cab shape) and the end product is shown in this view of No.14686 Urquart Castle at Inverness box on 18th August 1939, the only known pre-war colour view of this class. The livery was lined black (there is a trace of red lining visible on the tender in the original Dufay!) and the insignia can be seen to be the small 'Scottish' 10in gold numerals (above). (Pendragon Collection - Ref: LM86)

The next HR 4-6-0 design was another so-called 'goods' type, designed in 1917 by Cumming with 5ft 3in driving wheels and introduced, four each year, in 1918 and 1919. They were eventually known as 'Clan Goods' after the passenger version had appeared in 1919 - below - and as can be seen in this view, they too were used on passenger working; this is the down Wick Mail train about to depart from Inverness on 19th August 1939. The leading engine is Clan Goods No.17956 and the train engine is 'Small Ben' Class 4-4-0 No.14412 Ben Avon. The 4-6-0 has plain black livery with plain gold (actually gold shaded black) insignia. Like all the views taken on this occasion, the colour is not very strong and the engines are rather grimy, but the subject matter is sufficiently rare to merit inclusion. (Pendragon Collection - Ref: LM91)

This second view of the down Wick Mail preparing for departure on 19th August 1939 offers slightly more detail of the 4-4-0 and also gives a good impression of the Highland TPO No.30323, not to mention the Highland infrastructure, still strongly evident - note, for example, the HR signal arms and huge finials. The livery of the 4-4-0 should have been lined black, but honesty compels one to admit that this is not confirmable! (Pendragon Collection - Ref: LM87)

As with the Jones Goods and Castle 4-6-0s, Cumming also offered a passenger version of his goods design. Four were built in 1919 (another four in 1921) and they were all named after Highland Clans. Like all the HR 4-6-0 designs they were fine robust engines and although rather few in number (and definitely non-standard), they did not go to the scrapyard, as did many other small classes, during the 1930s. In fact, they were deemed useful enough to be moved by the LMS to the Oban line, where they proved vastly more effective than the feeble, albeit pretty looking Pickersgill 191 Class - above. This picture of No.14765 Clan Stewart *was taken at Oban in August 1939 and shows it in company with one of the still quite new Stanier Class 5s (possibly No.5004) and a pair of 0-6-0s, the nearer of which is identified as ex-CR Drummond 'Jumbo' No.17393. The Clan is in lined black (again there can only be seen traces of lining on the tender) and like many other views from this period, the general state of cleanliness was not of the best.* (Colour-Rail - Ref: LM4)

The Clans began to be withdrawn in 1943 but two reached BR, only one of which was to receive its BR number. No.14767 Clan Mackinnon *was the engine concerned and this fine portrait shot, taken at Aviemore in July 1946, shows the engine in the condition in which it was received by BR. The livery is now unlined black - as indeed were most LMS engines after the war - but the presence of the name and the red shaded insignia (which again seem to be the 'Scottish' style gold not yellow) give a touch of distinction. Note the lack of smokebox numberplate; as with the LNWR engines, so too on the Scottish pre-1923 types, this 'standard' LMS feature was more often missing than present after the livery changes of 1928.* (J.M.Jarvis - Ref: LM71)

The 2-6-0 wheel arrangement was rare on LMS lines in 1923, there being only a handful from the CR and G&SWR (essentially 'lengthened' 0-6-0s) before the 1927 introduction of the 'Horwich Moguls'. They were usually called 'Crabs' by most enthusiasts but this name was not often used by enginemen. Stanier developed the design with taper boiler in 1933 and Ivatt added two new types in 1946, but this is the only pre-BR colour view we have found of any of them, apart from an example in the background of the 1936 view of Sturdee at Rugby (above). This image from July 1946 shows 'Horwich' 2-6-0 No.2724 piloting an up express at Wymondham Junction. This was not an unknown type of duty for these engines, especially at weekends, but it was far less common than the express and fitted freight work for which they were primarily designed. The train is a typical 'mix' of Stanier and earlier LMS standard stock but the leading coach is a 'double brake ended' composite of LNWR origin. The train engine is ex-MR compound 4-4-0 No.1019 and both locomotives are in plain black 'utility' (wartime?) livery, very probably with the yellow/red insignia. Before 1940, they would have been lined black and crimson lake respectively (H.N.James - Ref: LM15)

All LMS constituents made extensive use of 4-4-0s but of the larger systems, only the Midland used them exclusively and it was the Midland compound 4-4-0 which soon came to dominate the rest, being adopted by the LMS as the first new 'standard' express passenger type as early as 1924. They were very fine engines but arguably too small for the heavier West Coast trains and double-heading was common - regular practice on the MR but anathema to all true LNWR men! By 1923, the MR had 45 in service, Nos.1000-44 (most MR engines kept their old numbers after 1922). Most of them were superheated (the rest soon followed) and this version became the LMS standard. Happily, a number of good pre-war images have survived of both variants and this first picture shows two ex-Midland engines, Nos.1007 and 1017 typically double-heading at St Albans in 1938; and it is only a down local! The leading engine still wears the older gold insignia (black shaded) with 10in figures on the cab, while the train engine carries the newer 1937 yellow/red insignia with 12in numerals. The train engine also has a replacement Stanier chimney. The tenders differ considerably which was something of a feature of this class. The leading engine has a hybrid style (LMS tank, MR underframe) while the train engine has a Deeley Midland tender, a design from which stemmed the later Midland/early LMS standard type. The carriages visible are LMS standard non-corridors of Stanier vintage. ((Colour-Rail - Ref: LM11)

The LMS built no fewer than 190 new compounds during 1924-7 and Stanier agreed to another five in 1932, thus making a total of 240, the largest class of three-cylinder compounds anywhere in the world and Britain's largest class of 4-4-0s of any type. The LMS examples had the driving wheels reduced from 7ft to 6ft 9in, larger cylinders and, apart from the first 40 (Nos.1045-84), reduced height boiler mountings to enable them to 'clear' the LMS composite structure gauge; these engines (Nos.1085-199 and 900-39) also had the driving position moved from right to left, the latter being the preferred LMS position. This view shows a typical example from the main LMS standard series, No.1141, on which can be seen the left hand side reversing rod, the shorter chimney and the 'flattened' dome cover compared with the previous view. Seen at Crewe North in April 1937, the engine displays a rather tired red livery carrying the older gold insignia with black shading and paler yellow lining (the latter intended to 'match' the gold); it may have been due for an early repaint. The cab has large Midland type 14in numerals but after 1937, most compounds carried the 12in type, unless in the 9xx series when the 14in version was regularly retained. The tender is the Fowler LMS standard 3500 gallon type, used on most new engines until a year or two after Stanier's arrival on the scene. (J.P.Mullett - Ref: LM48)

This delightful view of ex-MR No.1014 was taken at Shrewsbury in 1938 with the new 1937 yellow/red insignia clearly seen. The chimney is still tall but is a Stanier replacement of the original and the smokebox has acquired an external pipe for the exhaust steam injector (a common modification). The picture also gives a very good impression of one version of the hybrid tenders mentioned earlier. In the 1930s, it was found that many old MR tender chassis were still quite sound although the tanks were life-expired. The LMS therefore fitted the new standard Fowler tank to the old MR chassis. Unfortunately, as far as the aesthetics were concerned, the old chassis were often longer in wheelbase than those of the new standard tenders, so the new tanks stopped short at the rear - well seen here. (The late P.B.Whitehouse - Ref: LM26)

Yet another engine-tender combination was to couple a Midland tender to one of the LMS standard engines. In this lovely view at Scarborough in August 1938, early LMS standard compound No.1048 is paired with a a Deeley pattern tender of the type which was also fitted to many of the MR engines and was one of those with a longer wheelbase than the later LMS standard type. The engine has the RH drive configuration and tall chimney of the MR series but the flattened dome is to LMS standard pattern. The livery displays 1937 style lettering and numbers and the Dufaycolour original has really captured the richness of the red shade - see also the remarks above concerning the Jubilees. To have been photographed at Scarborough (LNER), the locomotive would almost certainly have arrived there in connection with a summer special working. (Pendragon Collection - Ref: LM83)

This second quite splendid broadside view makes an excellent comparison with the previous picture. Taken at Derby in 1938, it shows LMS standard LH drive No.1111, ex-works with yellow/red insignia and coupled to a Deeley ex-MR tender of a different style to that shown with No.1048. This time, the tender is one of those which were rebuilt well before 1923 from former Johnson bogie tenders soon after the MR introduced water troughs. They had very slightly higher side sheets and a rounded 'turn-under' to the tank just below the side valance. Once again, the red colour has reproduced very well. (Philip Colebourn Collection)

ABOVE: *Though found system-wide, the compounds were essentially Midland engines and this view really sums it up - a pair of them double heading out of St Pancras with an unidentified down express in 1938. The individual engines cannot be identified either, though their chimneys suggest they are both LMS standard types. By this time, double-headed 4-4-0 working was less common on the Midland main line than it once had been, there being plenty of new 5XP 4-6-0s available. But the scene has a timeless quality - change the Stanier coaches for Midland Clerestories and the picture could well date from 1918, so little has the scene changed. Period atmosphere abounds in the shape of Midland signals and signal box, not to mention the famous gasholder; while the picture itself is one of several in this book which has an almost 'oil-painted' quality to it, typical of much of the best Dufaycolour of the time.* (Pendragon Collection - Ref: LM86)

OPPOSITE, ABOVE: *The Midland had many other classes of 4-4-0, not least the Class 2P inside cylinder type which also spawned a successor in the LMS standard fleet; but apart from the compounds, this is the only early colour image to have been located. It does, however, show a more than usually interesting type: the Class 3P 'Belpaire'. The name may seem odd to some, given that nearly all MR 4-4-0s had Belpaire fireboxes when the LMS received them, but this class took its name because when the pioneer example was built in 1900, it was the first Midland engine to have such a feature. All told, 80 were built by Johnson and Deeley between 1900 and 1907 and there were many small (and not so small) variations. The later survivors were all superheated and many reckoned that the LMS would have done better to develop this type rather than the 2P. The picture, all the more remarkable because it is a 'freeze-frame' extract from a 16mm cine source, shows No.762 leaving Oxford (Rewley Road) with a Bletchley train in September 1947. The livery is unlined black with yellow/red insignia and the engine is one of the 1907 Deeley series.* (The late P.B.Whitehouse - Ref: LM59)

OPPOSITE, BELOW: *Like the MR, the LNWR had a formidable number of 4-4-0s but, as with so many other interesting types, they mostly eluded contemporary colour photographers, so once again, this is may well be the only surviving pre-war image. Taken at Coventry in 1939 its interest matches its rarity, for it demonstrates that in spite of ruthless standardisation, the LMS still operated many services with old stock well into the 1930s and beyond. Here is a quite lengthy stopping train consisting wholly of pre-1923 coaches and headed by a 35 year old locomotive of celebrated origin: superheated 'Precursor' class 4-4-0 No.25319* Bucephalus. *The engine was built in 1904 as the very last of its class and by the time of this picture, it had acquired the typical LMS modifications (cab, belpaire firebox &c) already described for the Prince of Wales 4-6-0s.*

The Precursors were good engines, doing much hard work in LNWR days, along with their successors, the even better 'George the Fifth' type, developed from the Precursors which they much resembled. But they found less favour in LMS days and most had gone by the late 1930s, No.25319 being a late survivor until 1940. Even so, it carries lined black livery with shaded 1937 insignia and is in reasonable condition. The stock is an interesting assemblage, consisting of a strengthening LNWR 50ft 'cove' roof non-corridor third of 1906 vintage at the front, followed by a four coach set of ex-Midland Railway 48ft low-roof non-corridors of about the same age. Two high roof LNWR non-corridors are to the rear and there may be more out of camera shot. (Philip Colebourn Collection)

OPPOSITE, ABOVE: *The 2-4-0 was a common Victorian passenger type but had been mostly superseded by the 4-4-0 well before the 20th Century, so it is remarkable that on such a standardised railway as the LMS, two typical mid-Victorian examples should have survived to be photographed in colour; needless to say, they were both ex-MR and this first picture shows the older of them simmering in the sunshine at Bedford in 1938: veteran double-framed Kirtley 2-4-0 No.20002 (MR/LMS No.2 until 1934), dating from 1866! The livery is a well-maintained lined black with the red/yellow 1937 insignia, though the smaller than standard numerals could well have been hand painted. This is a famous engine for it was destined to be the last surviving Kirtley locomotive and as a tribute to this fine pioneering engineer, is fittingly preserved in the National Collection, now displaying its pre-1907 MR No.158A. Unfortunately, when it was preserved, some foolish and unidentified person decided to couple it to the last surviving Kirtley tender, which was a type it never trailed when in the external 'locomotive' form shown here. The engine carries visible evidence of rebuilding both by Johnson and Deeley and it would have been impossible to change it back to 1866 condition. So for those who have seen the preserved No.158A, they might be interested in seeing what it should really look like!! (Philip Colebourn Collection)*

OPPOSITE, BELOW: *The LMS passenger tender engine section of this book is concluded with a fine and recently discovered picture taken at Wellingborough on 28th July 1938. The camera has not completely 'stopped' the movement (a real problem with the slow speed colour film of the time - or was the photographer trying to 'pan' the shot?), but the colour rendition is excellent and the picture is packed full of historical interest. The engine is 2-4-0 No.20267 (MR/LMS No.267 until c.1936), built in 1881 as one of Johnson's famous '1400 Class' introduced in 1879. Most longer term survivors of the class were rebuilt with belpaire fireboxes as seen here. It carries the lined black livery with 1937 style characters.*

The train carries Class 2 (ordinary/stopping passenger) headcode but the first two coaches are both corridors. Leading is a former Midland brake third (one of only a few MR corridors with full elliptical roof) followed by an early LMS corridor composite from the mid-1920s. The next vehicle (just visible on the original) cannot be determined but is likely to be another corridor third brake, making the formation a typical three coach LMS 'Inter-Corridor' set. The first carriage seems to be in simplified LMS livery but unless the camera is lying, the yellow/black/yellow lining appears on both upper and lower waist mouldings - a hitherto unknown livery variant and not 'according to book'. The second coach is in fully lined 1923-34 livery (the centrally positioned 'LMS' only lasted until 1930) and the carriage in the siding is a steel panelled 57ft open third dating from 1931 with the modified post-1930 version of full LMS livery - ie no waist 'panel'. (Pendragon Collection - Ref: LM89)

BELOW: *It has to be said that this picture nearly 'missed the cut', as the golfers might say; but it is the only known pre-BR colour picture of a Stanier Class 8F 2-8-0 at work and early colour views of any LMS freight types are thin on the ground at the best of times! The engine is No.8429 working a down express freight at White Waltham (GWR) in April 1947 and this adds to the interest. During the war, all four British railways had built LMS Class 8Fs (the design was selected as a War Department standard freight type) and except for those which went directly into the WD inventory, all carried LMS series running numbers. This example was built by the GWR in 1943 and was used on that system, officially 'on loan' from LMS stock. Close examination reveals the lack of front numberplate and, though not visible here, this group carried painted numbers on the front buffer plank in the GWR style. It is also worth noting that the GWR later used the flanging blocks for the 8F boilers for its own 'County' Class 4-6-0 - maybe the Swindon origins of the 8F's designer had something to do with it! (H.N.James - Ref: LM2)*

One reason for the relatively small number of Class 8F 2-8-0s on LMS lines in the pre-war years was undoubtedly because of the considerable attention which had been given after 1922 to the progressive development of the LNWR 'Super D' 0-8-0 type and which Stanier allowed to continue. It therefore became almost a 'standard' LMS class in its own right and was the shining exception to the usual scrapyard fate of many LNWR locomotives. The 'Super D' nomenclature came from the Class G1 via an earlier classification 'Class D Superheater'. The full story of development and rebuilding in both LNWR and LMS days is too complex to cover here (it is well recorded elsewhere, however). Suffice to say that by the late 1930s, all the surviving LNWR 0-8-0s were either G1 (Power Class 6F) or G2/G2A (Power Class 7F). The G2s were simply G1s with higher boiler pressure, the G2A variation being used for those rebuilt to G2 from earlier types, and it is a G1 which is shown in this fine portrait study at Bletchley in June 1938.

No.9162 was built by the LNWR as Class G1 and remained thus, though many others were rebuilt to G2A by the LMS. Externally, the two types were much the same, though as with other LNWR classes, belpaire or round top fireboxes (as on this engine) could be seen with either and all were given the modified 'LMS' cab shape seen here. The livery was unlined black but the insignia were a Crewe speciality. It was customary for freight engines to be painted in the erecting hop at Crewe (it saved time and money) and transfer insignia were expensive, so Crewe made outline stencils to the LMS standard shape and handpainted the insignia in 'straw' colour paint. They usually had 14in numerals as seen here but there were exceptions. (L.Hanson - Ref: LM42)

ABOVE: *This second view of a Class 4F is also more than usually interesting. Taken at Scarborough in August 1938, it shows a ten-coach holiday working heading back to LMS territory behind No.4183, one of the earlier LMS standard examples with RH drive. The engine still has cylinder tail rod housings and may be carrying plain gold insignia (which preceded the 1937 yellow/red). Weekend holiday duty was a quite common summer occupation for many types of locomotive, including goods engines (provided they could work the vacuum brake); and their relatively high tractive effort, compared with the older and smaller passenger types which might be the only available alternative, enabled them to cope with the heavier loads which such trains could often generate; top speed was less important than getting there and back with adequate engine power!*

The train is a typical LMS mid-period mixture of gangwayed stock. A cove roof 57ft LNWR double-ended brake composite of c.1906 vintage leads. It has red ends, which infers fully lined livery, and may even have offered the only first class accommodation on the train - all of twelve seats! It is followed by two seven-compartment LNWR corridor thirds in two further styles. Next come two LMS standard 56 seat open thirds plus a kitchen car, so clearly the train was going far enough for full meal service to be offered. The rest of the train cannot be fully determined but may well have consisted of more open thirds and a third brake at the rear. (Philip Colebourn Collection)

LEFT: *The Midland Class 4F 0-6-0 was adopted as standard by the LMS and became the most numerous single type of engine ever to carry LMS identity: including the 197 MR-built examples (five of them for the Somerset and Dorset), no fewer that 772 were built (there were, of course, 842 Class 5s and 852 Class 8Fs but many of the latter were either WD owned and/or lost overseas; while 100 of the Class 5s were built by BR). Even so, pre-BR colour views of 4Fs are rare so it is fortunate that one of them should give such a sparkling (certainly untypical!) impression of these ubiquitous engines as does this view of No.4413, taken ex-works at Derby after full overhaul in July 1946. The engine is one of many LMS standard examples built with LH drive in 1925-8 (the first LMS-built examples had RH drive, c.f the compound 4-4-0s) and just about the only visible change from its original state is the removal of the tail rod housings on the front buffer plank and a replacement Stanier pattern chimney. The livery is 100% definitive, leaving no room for doubt about the 1937 yellow and red insignia, used on most fully repainted engines for the rest of the LMS period, even after the 1946 style had been adopted. The latter was confined to new and repainted express types, some new Class 5s and 2-6-4Ts (plus a few repainted examples) and the new Ivatt designs.* (H.N.James - Ref: LM14)

The Class 4F could trace its ancestry back to the original double framed Kirtley 0-6-0s, the first of them introduced in 1850, which set parameters of wheelbase and cylinder layout which ever afterwards remained the MR standard, and were to be found on the last 4Fs of 1941! The last survivor of this venerable range of Kirtley 0-6-0s was No.22630 which actually reached BR becoming BR No.58110. It was to Kirtley's later 1863 design(!) and is seen here in steam at Bournville shed (one of the last homes of the type) in June 1946. The livery is unlined black with yellow/red insignia and the tender is of Kirtley pattern with the slightly extended and flush rivetted tank side panels.
(J.M.Jarvis - Ref: LM29)

Though somewhat restrained in colour and not 'pinpoint' sharp, this 'total scene', taken at Willesden Junction in 1939, contains much of interest. In the centre, a Belpaire-boilered 'Cauliflower' is leaving Willesden with an up empty carriage stock working and is seen crossing from the down side of the line, across the fast lines to the up slow track. The full formation cannot be determined, nor the actual working for which it was intended, but the nearest pair of coaches can clearly be identified as a Stanier corridor third plus one of the recently introduced Stanier 62ft brake composites. Next is a third brake which is likely to be the rear vehicle of the main train, the nearest pair obviously forming a through portion destined to be detached from the rear of the train en route. In the right foreground, one of the still quite new Stanier 69ft first class sleeping cars stands in the siding alongside the south carriage shed - note the low height 'servicing platforms' between the carriage sidings. Note too that even in 1939, all visible infrastructure and signals are still firmly LNWR. (The late Sydney Perrier, courtesy C.S.Perrier - Ref: LM78)

LEFT: *The LNWR was also a great user of 0-6-0s, but Webb introduced the 0-8-0 in the late 19th Century and in consequence, few new LNWR 0-6-0s were built after that time. Webb's last design of 0-6-0 dated from 1887 and many of them came to the LMS, a fair number enjoying a longer LMS life than many other inherited LNWR types. One such is seen here, No.8592 at Bletchley coal stage in June 1938 - and note the LNER coal wagon! The engines were familiarly known as 'Crested Goods' in LNWR days, because they carried the company crest on the centre splasher; but they were more familiarly known as 'Cauliflowers' since this was the visual impression given by the crest when seen at any distance! This name remained with them to the end. Like many LNWR engines in LMS days, they could be seen with either Belpaire or round top fireboxes and it is one of the older round tops which is featured here. The livery is interesting, for the 14in numerals are of Midland pattern and have been applied in transfer form - compare the shape of the '9' with the handpainted version shown on the 0-8-0 on a previous page, photographed on the same occasion. They are also gold (gilt) not pale yellow which could indicate that Crewe was using up pre-1936 transfer stocks of the type used on Royal Scots from 1928-36. However, Crewe also began to make more use of transfer insignia with the intermediate lined black livery during the immediate pre-war years, an aspect discussed already, so perhaps there was a slight change of policy.* (L.Hanson - Ref: LM44)

This third view of No.12510 shows the engine at Moor Row again in August 1947, now fitted with replacement LYR Belpaire boiler - which gives quite a different character to the locomotive. The insignia are still unshaded and clearly not of the 1937 yellow/red variety; whether they are gold (gilt) or pale yellow cannot be confirmed. But it is known that Horwich made widespread use of unshaded (black shaded) transfers on all freight engines and may have had a very large stock of the pre-1937 type. Note too that with the LYR type boiler, the front numberplate was omitted - a typical feature of LYR locomotives too. While on this subject, it is sad to note that apart from the picture of a 4-6-0 offered earlier in this chapter, this is the only other early colour view suitable for reproduction of anything which shows LYR features! (H.N.James - Ref: LM10)

OPPOSITE, ABOVE: *This picture is one of a remarkable set of colour views taken at an unusual time (in the snow), at an uncommon location and in a surprising year, the winter of 1941. Two of them feature the same locomotive, and a rare one at that time: Furness Railway 0-6-0 No.12510. In this first view, the engine is seen outside the shed at Moor Row in February 1941 with an unidentified 17in 'Coal' engine outside the shed and some nice 'railway furniture' scattered around. The engine itself was to Pettigrew's final 0-6-0 design for the FR, fifteen of which were built from 1913. Classified 3F, they enjoyed a much longer active life in LMS days than most small non-standard classes, arguably because it was possible to fit them with replacement LYR pattern superheated Belpaire boilers. Six actually reached BR and the example illustrated was the last to go (as BR No.52510 in 1957). It is seen here with original FR boiler and carrying very clean plain black livery with unshaded insignia. The latter are likely to have been plain gold, though plain yellow is not impossible. By this time, Horwich was shopping the engines and had a large supply of plain gold transfers (actually black shaded) dating back to the pre-1936 livery when all goods engines had plain black characters.* (Pendragon Collection - Ref: LM93)

OPPOSITE, BELOW: *Though from a separate source, this second picture at Moor Row was certainly taken on the same occasion and by the same (unknown) photographer as the last and shows the engine attached to its train, prior to moving into the station. No.12510 is carrying a passenger headlamp and the train is a fairly tidy set of early non-corridor stock. At first glance these could well appear to be of LNWR origin, and some of them may indeed be so; but the central location and shape of guard's lookout on the leading vehicle, together with the roof shape and configuration of the second, reveal that these two, at least, are of Furness Railway type and the whole train may be thus composed. If so, the ensemble was a fairly remarkable survivor from an earlier generation. The service is not known but it may have been for workmen.* (Colour-Rail - Ref: LM9)

The large passenger tank was an important element of the LMS scene but again, the availability of early pictures is poor. Fortunately, those which have come to light are mostly of good quality and show different types. In this view, taken at St Albans City station in May 1939, the 'grandad' of all modern 2-6-4Ts is seen in the form of Fowler Class 4P No.2328, fairly newly repainted in lined black livery with the bright yellow/red insignia. The 14in numerals were the norm for this class, there being plenty of room for them. The Fowler 2-6-4Ts introduced the wheel arrangement to the LMS in 1927 and the design was one of the unqualified successes of the pre-Stanier period. They were outstandingly good engines and could run 'like the wind', especially on the outer suburban services of the kind on which No.2328 is likely to be engaged. The engine is one of the early examples with 'open sided' cab. The last examples had a variant with side windows and cab doors - much as on the succeeding Stanier type. (The late Sydney Perrier, courtesy C.S.Perrier - Ref: LM76)

Stanier naturally continued the 2-6-4T and equally predictably gave it a taper boiler. The first 37 examples had three cylinders but from No.2537 upwards he reverted to the two-cylinder layout of the Fowler engines - and for once, his engines showed no great improvement over the parallel boiler predecessor; both were very good. In due course, rather more Stanier 2-6-4Ts were built than the Fowler type and many of them came into service from new with the short-lived 1936 style sans-serif insignia and matching sans-serif smokebox numberplates. One such is shown here: No.2550, at Nottingham in June 1937. Most of Stanier's two-cylinder 2-6-4Ts were built new with domed boilers and separate top feed, the experiment with domeless boilers, discussed earlier, having ceased. In this form, they paved the way (via Fairburn's final LMS design) for the BR Standard Class 4 2-6-4Ts. (The late J.A.Whaley - Ref: LM54)

In 1930, the LMS introduced a Class 3P 2-6-2 passenger tank, intended to be a sort of scaled-down version of the successful 2-6-4T, but it turned out to be a feeble performer and not particularly well received. Why Stanier continued with the type will never be fully known, but he did try to improve the concept. They were better than the parallel boiler engines and eventually there were almost twice as many of them, but they were never 'world beaters'. However, like so many Stanier designs, they were extremely well proportioned, attractive looking engines whose character is well caught by this superb shot of No.91 at Derby in July 1938, newly ex-works after a repaint with yellow/red insignia and large 14in numerals. The engine is one of the earlier examples with domeless boilers (Nos.71-144). (Colour-Rail - Ref: LM13)

One of the most important groups of pre-standard 'large' passenger tank engines on the LMS was the celebrated series of 4-4-2 'Tilbury Tanks'. Their origins went back to the independent London, Tilbury and Southend Railway and both the Midland (which purchased the LT&SR in 1912) and the LMS continued to develop the type. The last new examples came out under LMS auspices as late as 1930 and were given Nos.2151-60 (ie in the former MR series in numerical succession to the older engines); one of these is seen in this view at Plaistow shed in August 1937, sporting what at first could seem to be a quite fascinating livery. Appropriately enough, it is lined black, but the lining appears to be blue and not vermilion, the official style. The only explanation for this which can be hazarded is that pre-war Agfa (the original film in this case) was notoriously liable to fading and the lining is probably faded red. Another point of interest is that this is the only known contemporary colour view which clearly indicates the nature of the attractive 'countershaded' transfers which the LMS used on most of its lined black engines between 1929 and 1936 (and on a few red ones too). The plain gold (black shaded?) numerals on the adjoining Class 3F 0-6-0T No.7497 are also worthy of note; they were absolutely typical of the pre-1937 situation. (L.Hanson - Ref: LM41)

The LMS inherited a great variety of smaller passenger tanks but this and the next 'freeze frame' 16mm cine extracts are the only early colour views of any of them - and even then they are technically 'BR', having been taken in 1948. This first example was taken near Dudley Port and shows Webb LNWR 0-6-2 'Watford' tank No.6922 shunting coal wagons, some of which still show vestigal signs of their earlier (pre-war) decorative private owner liveries. Webb designed two types of 0-6-2T and this version, the larger wheeled of the two, was generally regarded as the passenger type (hence 'Watford' tanks), though 'mixed traffic' might have been a more appropriate. The 'livery' is basically filth which, along with the next few views, only too clearly reveals that the so-called 'colourful' pre-BR period was 'anything but' in the difficult years during and after the war. The chances are that the insignia on the engine (Midland pattern numbers) date from before the war - see next view. (The late P.B.Whitehouse - Ref: LM60)

This next 'freeze frame' was taken at Coalport, also in 1948, and shows Webb LNWR 2-4-2T No.6601 leaving with a local for Madeley Market and Wellington. Happily, it is sharp enough to reveal that, like the previous example, the 14in numerals are the Midland style transfer type in gold rather than the painted 'Crewe' standard form in pale yellow - see earlier captions to the LNWR freight tender engines. Many of the 2-4-2Ts and Watford Tanks did receive lined black livery before the war but this one is clearly plain black. What cannot be determined is whether the engine still wears a pre-war coat of paint or if it was repainted later; the former seems marginally more likely. The visible coach is a Stanier period non-corridor in simple livery. (The late P.B.Whitehouse - Ref: LM61)

ABOVE: *This much better quality view, taken in 1948 in the late evening sunshine at Copmanthorpe, near York, shows No.7987, one of the celebrated but none-too-successful LMS 2-6-0+0-6-2 Garratt locomotives - classified as 'freight tank engines' by the company. The Garratt idea was very sound and usually very successful, but there was too much interference in their design by reactionary forces at Derby and the LMS version fell far short of the standard of excellence which the type achieved when used overseas. Nevertheless they could replace two conventional 0-6-0s (which was the intention) and they pulled some heavy trains: this one is empty ironstone hoppers from Skinningrove to Desborough and the engine would almost certainly have brought a similar but loaded train northwards prior to this return working to LMS territory. The livery is plain black and the insignia, with numerals at both ends of the locomotive, is of the handpainted Crewe style. The engine is working bunker (or 'hind end') first, a direction not enjoyed by the crew because of the tendency of coal dust to swirl into the cab, though the enclosed rotating coal bunker helped to some extent. It may even be that the locomotive was arranged this way so that it worked chimney ('fore end') first when the train was loaded.* (E.Sanderson - Ref: LM90)

The larger wheeled LNWR 0-6-2Ts (opposite) were regarded as passenger types (and put into the LMS passenger tank number series for the ex-LNWR fleet), though they often handled freight. In like manner, the smaller-wheeled 0-6-2 'Coal' tanks were regarded as freight engines (and put in the LMS freight tank number series for ex-LNWR engines) and they often handled passenger trains! One such engine clearly earmarked for passenger duty was No.7833, seen here fitted for motor train (push-pull) working - note the two vacuum pipes above the buffer beam. This is yet another 'freeze frame' from 1948 and was taken at Nantybwch on the old penetrating LNWR line to the head of the South Wales valleys. The Coal tanks, dating from 1881, were very useful machines and far more resilient than many LNWR types. Happily, an example is preserved, one of far too few representatives of what was, prior to 1923, Britain's largest single fleet of steam locomotives. (The late P.B.Whitehouse - Ref: LM69)

ABOVE: *It is curious that although the LNWR locomotives fared far worse than their Midland equivalents after 1922, far more of them seem to have been photographed in colour during the period covered by this survey, and this one is especially interesting: Webb 2-4-0T No.6428, dating from 1877. There was also a 2-4-2T version of this type, 50 of which were rebuilt from 2-4-0Ts and both varieties were often referred to as 'Chopper' tanks. The example illustrated was by far the longest lasting of its type and survived to BR as No.58092, having been, for a short period, 'duplicated' as LMS 26428 so as to allow for new Ivatt 2-6-0s in the 64xx series. One reason for its long survival was because, along with other remaining 2-4-0Ts, it was transferred to work on the unique Cromford and High Peak line, a mineral railway which traversed the uplands of the Peak District to which it gained access via a combination of horrendously steep adhesion-worked locomotive sections and rope-worked inclines. The engine was photographed in 1943 at the foot of the Middleton Incline. To reach the top of Sheep Pasture, from whence it worked to Middleton 'bottom', it had to be rope-hauled. It was numbered in the LMS(LNWR) passenger tank series but it seems more fitting to put it with the freight tanks. In this view, its number is handpainted in the Crewe manner with tiny 'LMS' on the bunker side.* (Philip Colebourn Collection)

OPPOSITE, ABOVE: *This is another rarity from the group of images taken at Moor Row in the snow during February 1941, already mentioned. This time, the subject is the last surviving Furness Railway 0-6-0T No.11553, standing in front of 0-6-0 No.12510 and presumably taken on the same occasion (see earlier captions). No.11553 was the first of ten examples to a Pettigrew design dating from 1910 and scrapped in 1943 some seven years after all the others had gone. It was used on the Lakeside branch in later years, some considerable distance from the location of this picture. The livery is plain black with (almost certainly) plain gold insignia.* (Pendragon Collection - Ref: LM94)

OPPOSITE, BELOW: *The LMS survey is concluded with a pair of pictures which show a long-lived type from a system not so far mentioned - the North London Railway. By the time of the Grouping, the NLR was a subsidiary of the LNWR and its most common locomotives were a series of distinctive 4-4-0Ts which did not long survive the 1923 amalgamations. However, its robust outside-cylindered 0-6-0Ts, dating from 1879, fared very much better and these pictures are typical. In the first view, No.27509 (it had been No.7509 in the ex-LNWR freight tank series until the 1934 renumbering of the LMS standard 0-6-0Ts) is seen on home ground at Devons Road shed (ex-NLR) in August 1937. As can be seen, there was none too much space for the LMS insignia which, albeit degraded, seems to have been of the countershaded gold style already mentioned in connection with the Tilbury 4-4-2T (above). The figures are the 12in variety.* (L.Hanson - Ref: LM45)

The second picture shows the last survivor, No.27527, now very far away from the industrial environment of London's dockland and working 'light engine' up the 1:14 Hopton Incline of the aforementioned C&HPR, the steepest adhesion worked line in Britain. Photographed in September 1943, it was sent there c.1932 and remained until 1960, becoming the last of its class (fifteen of the original thirty had actually reached BR). It was clearly suited to this role and is now preserved as NLR No.92 on the Bluebell Railway. In this picture, it carries unshaded insignia, this time with 14in Midland style numerals - quite probably in gold. It is even possible that the extra '2' was simply transferred in front of the old number when the engine went onto the duplicate list in July 1936 and that it had not been repainted after that date. (Colour-Rail - Ref: LM8)

CHAPTER TWO

LONDON AND NORTH EASTERN RAILWAY

To the historian, the survival of much elderly equipment - and the fact that, of necessity, it had to be kept in good order - made the LNER a fascinating company to study, a fact well exemplified in this introductory picture.

Taken at Cambridge on 11th June 1938, it shows, in front of a train of more modern Gresley corridor stock, ex-GER Class E4 2-4-0 No.7490 with the Mildenhall Branch train of four ex-GER six-wheel coaches plus a van. The branch set proper consists of the middle three coaches, all 34ft 6in non-corridor stock dating from 1892-6 and built for main line use. In 1922-3, some of these were converted for 'conductor guard' working on less prosperous branch lines by opening up interiors, sealing up most doors save those at the ends and providing gangways. Three types were involved, all seen here: six-compartment third, six-compartment composite, three compartment brake third. The sealed up doors are readily visible. The first coach, on what was destined to be its last revenue journey, is a five compartment third (ex-second), originally built in 1899 for Liverpool Street outer-suburban use. The final van is a former GER six-wheel 'General Van' with sliding doors.

The locomotive is the most celebrated member of an excellent class of so-called 'Intermediate' 2-4-0s, deliberately designed for mixed traffic use in 1895. It is, very appropriately, finished in the 'intermediate' LNER lined black livery and obviously well cared for. It became LNER No.7802 in 1942, LNER No.2785 under the 1946 scheme and as BR No.62785, ran on to become the last British 2-4-0 in service. Withdrawn at the end of 1959, it was selected for preservation in the National Collection, restored at Stratford and given the full GER 'Royal Blue' livery, bearing its original GER No.490. (Philip Colebourn Collection)

An Introduction to the LNER

The LNER has been very fortunate in its historians. There are excellent accounts in print of the company and its rolling stock and a vast literature on the whole of its locomotive fleet, particularly the design and performance of its more prestigious locomotives. In consequence, the LNER is often perceived purely in terms of its streamlined trains, Gresley pacifics and high profile publicity. These were indeed a vital part of the story but in relation to the company as a whole, they represented but the visible part of the 'Company Iceberg', for the truth was that the LNER was the least wealthy of the Big Four, operating more old equipment, relative to the total, than any of the others. Indeed, it has been calculated that in the mid-1930s, the LNER alone accounted for over 50% of the remaining four- and six-wheel coaches left in service in all of Britain - see introductory picture.

The railway ran down the eastern side of Scotland and England from the Great North of Scotland Railway territory, north and east of a line between Aberdeen and Inverness, to London itself. On the way, the next railway which came under LNER ownership was the North British, Scotland's largest single pre-group system. This stretched from Aberdeen in the north to the Scottish border, with a few penetrating branches into England, not to mention one of the main Edinburgh-Glasgow routes and the famous West Highland line from Glasgow to Fort William and Mallaig. The NBR main line to the south made an end-on junction at Berwick with the North Eastern, which constituent of the LNER held a virtual territorial monopoly east of the Pennines (north of the Humber estuary), having amalgamated with the Hull and Barnsley Railway just before the main grouping.

The remaining three constituents of the LNER were largely contained in the area from Yorkshire to the south. The Great Central Railway, which had been the Manchester Sheffield and Lincolnshire until 1897, re-named itself because it had promoted the last main line to London, thus extending its territory southwards from Sheffield via Nottingham and Leicester in a grand expansion which, if truth be told, was hardly necessary even at the time it was built; and it was often known as the 'Sheffield' to the very end. The Great Northern main line ran from London to Leeds and Bradford via Doncaster (with many important branches in the area north of Peterborough, particularly in Lincolnshire) while the Great Eastern Railway held a rather similar territorial monopoly in East Anglia to that of the NER further north. In addition, of course, there were numerous joint operations, some involving LNER constituents only, others taking the form of co-operation with different members of the 'Big Four'.

With the exception of the GNSR and H&BR fleet, it has been possible to find colour examples from all the principal LNER constituents for this survey and also to embrace a considerable variety of LNER locations and engine types. If there is a preponderance of passenger classes to be seen, this is no more than the result of factors mentioned in the introduction; but overall, the LNER, if only by chance, seems to have been better served by the colour photographers of the day than the rest of the 'Big Four'. And although the principal types dominate, quite a number of rare and unusual prototypes make their appearance

As many will know, the LNER renumbered its locomotives systematically in 1946. In cases where it is thought helpful in context, both pre- and post-1946 numbers are given in the caption information.

OPPOSITE, BELOW: *The original Gresley A4 pacific No.2509* Silver Link *departs from King's Cross with the 5.30pm 'Silver Jubilee' for Newcastle on 1st September 1937. Although by now almost two years since the first appearance of both locomotive and train they are obviously still a keen source of interest. The striking streamlined shape of No.2509 was brilliantly emphasised by its colour scheme, comprising three shades of grey: dark charcoal, battleship and silver. A few minor modifications had been made to the locomotive since it first entered revenue earning service. Most noteable in this view are the elongated standard numerals on the front of the streamlined casing, added in the summer of 1937. These replaced the standard sized numerals, silver shaded blue, used from the summer of 1936 on the silver A4s. No.2509 was one of five LNER locomotives to carry a silver grey livery. The four streamliners are well known, but a humble Doncaster works shunter of GNR origin, LNER class J55 0-6-0T No.4800, was used as a test bed for a variety of light silver-grey shades in August 1935.* (The late Sydney Perrier, courtesy C.S.Perrier - Ref: NE89)

ABOVE: *This classic pre-war shot shows* Silver Link *at Grantham in June 1937, hauling the up 'Flying Scotsman', mostly likely on a Saturday (either 5th, 12th or 19th). This view shows the longer buffers and rebuilt draw hook fitted in 1936 following a fatal accident; note also the smaller style figures on the front end. The dark charcoal grey painted on the front of the casing is swept back in a parabolic curve, whilst the valances and frames are painted in a lighter battleship grey, by now beginning to weather. The main body of the locomotive and tender is silver-grey. This colour was initially carried to the rain strip of the cab roof to match the corridor tender; it soon weathered in the same way as the white LNER carriage roof paint. The wheel tyres and rims were also picked out in battleship grey at first, although in this photograph they have been painted silver-grey overall. Another detail just visible is the painting of the axle boxes and springs of trailing axle and tender axles in dark charcoal or black to contrast with the battleship grey frames. The lettering was silver shaded blue. In December 1937 No.2509 was repainted in garter blue and given cast nameplates (it had briefly carried such in September 1935), while the last A4 to carry the silver livery was Gateshead based No.2511* Silver King, *which received garter blue in August 1938. The 'Flying Scotsman' headboard has painted lettering in Gill Sans characters. The original was painted in 1928 by Eric Gill himself. Note the tall GNR signal posts, already with replacement upper quadrant arms.* (J.A.Whaley - Ref: NE74)

ABOVE: *This rare view shows No.4482* Golden Eagle *on shed in December 1936 in the short-lived apple green livery. Brand new, having been allocated to King's Cross shed on 22nd December, it was the fifth A4 to be built and carried the standard LNER apple green livery for just over a year. In January 1938 it was repainted garter blue, by then adopted as the standard colour for A4s following its introduction on the new streamlined trains in 1937. The parabolic curve of black paint at the front of No.4482 was similar to the original silver locomotives, except that it was nearer the front edge of the casing. The next five A4s were also painted green, but the black paint was extended back to the first boiler cladding band and covered the whole smokebox area. This straight line completely destroyed the streamlined effect of the wedge front. Green livery was carried by nine members of the class, five having a modified black front (Nos.4483-7), whilst Nos. 4493-5 appeared carrying the same curve as No.4482. Red lining was applied to the corridor tender and trailing axle frames. It also edges the top and bottom of the streamlined valances. This engine was the first A4 to appear in service with cast nameplates placed on the smokebox casing, in like manner to the P2 2-8-2s.* (G.Ford - Ref: NE58)

OPPOSITE, ABOVE: *In 1937, the LNER introduced the soon to become famous 'garter blue' for the A4 pacifics to coincide with the start of two new streamlined services in Coronation year. The first five engines so treated (Nos.4488-92) were designated for the 'Coronation' service - see view of* Empire of India *(below) - while two more were allocated to the 'West Riding Limited' (Nos.4495-6). At the time of this decision, one of the chosen engines, No.4495 built in August 1937, had been running for a couple of weeks in apple green livery with the name* Great Snipe *but was then taken into shops for finishing in the new garter blue style. This view shows it in September 1937, just after emerging from shops in the new colour scheme, which included the stainless steel insignia and trimmings first seen on the five 'Coronation' series A4s. Soon after this view was taken it was renamed* Golden Fleece, *appropriate for its thematic connection (wool) with the industrial West Riding itself.* (Philip Colebourn Collection)

OPPOSITE, BELOW: *A4 4-6-2 No.4463* Sparrow Hawk *approaches New Barnet with the up 10.15 am from Edinburgh, due King's Cross 5.35 pm. The locomotive is in the standard LNER garter blue with dark red wheels, gold transfer characters plus cast nameplate; although it is only some nine months old there is already considerable evidence of weathering. No.4463 was based at Gateshead when this picture was taken in the summer of 1938 and would have hauled the train from Newcastle. The train itself conveyed through coaches from Glasgow, Aberdeen and Perth, with a further through coach from Glasgow to the south via the GC route having been dropped at Newcastle. The visible portion is made up of modern Gresley LNER stock but the surrounding environment is still predominantly Great Northern in character - note, for example, the somersault signals and platform lamps.* (The late Sydney Perrier, courtesy C.S.Perrier - Ref: NE91)

The onset of war did not immediately change the painting specifications on the LNER and it was November 1941 before instructions were given that all locomotives should be painted unlined black. A further economy followed in July 1942 when the lettering was altered from 'LNER' to 'NE'. A4 No.2510 Quicksilver was released from Doncaster works in early November 1941 with side valancing removed (another wartime change adopted for ease of maintenance) but still in garter blue livery; No.4464 Bittern, ex-works only a week later - was the first A4 to appear in plain black. Unsurprisingly, No.2510 was the last A4 running in pre-war blue which it carried until August 1943. The Grantham-based engine is seen here in wartime black hauling an up Leeds express north of Hatfield in August 1946. When it first appeared in black during 1943, the locomotive carried the abbreviated 'NE' on the tender, an economy which was reversed following a decision in February 1946. In consequence, No.2510 was released from general repair in April with LNER in full on the tender, as shown. Only a month after this picture was taken the engine was renumbered 15 under the post-war LNER scheme, so this view shows a very short-lived state. By mid 1946 the A4s were appearing once again in garter blue, although No.4496 had recieved the livery in September 1945 in honour of its renaming to Dwight D. Eisenhower. No.15 recieved its post war garter blue in October 1947. (Eric Bruton - Ref: NE100)

RIGHT: *This suberb evocation of the post war LNER scene shows one of the original garter blue A4s,* Empire of India *heading the down 'Flying Scotsman' at Newcastle Central in August 1947. Five locomotives (Nos.4488-92) were originally selected to haul the streamlined 'Coronation' express, were all given garter blue livery to match the blue shades of the train and received the names of the principal constituents of the Empire. Other special embellishments included the coat of arms of the country, carried below the number on the cab side, together with stainless steel lettering, numerals and trim - on the lower edges of valance and tender. Eventually ten members of the class carried stainless steel lettering. By the time this view was taken,* Empire of India *had undergone various changes. The trim has been removed along with the valance, whilst the cabside displays No.11 which it received when it was repainted garter blue in November 1946; it was formerly No.4490. The train itself is mostly Thompson steel panelled stock in 'ersatz teak' painted livery. The front coaches were soon replaced on this service by specially built pressure ventilated vehicles. The NER Tyneside electric stock in the background painted with Marlborough blue lower panels, separated by a black line from Quaker grey upper panels, is also worthy of note. The blue-grey livery dated from 1941 when it was adopted as being 'less conspicuous' in wartime than the original red and cream. These early NER units (released from North Tyneside lines) had been modernised in the mid-1930s for use on the newly electrified South Tyneside lines after the introduction of new LNER stock for North Tyneside.* (H.N.James - Ref: NE5)

A fine study of Class A1 Pacific No.2548 Galtee More *at the coaling plant of York shed in 1937. This shows off the post 1928 apple green livery to great advantage, ie. with 12in numerals on cabside rather than on the tender side. Note how quickly the red lining on the tops of the frames and running plate angle iron has weathered. Excepting minor details, the locomotive is largely in its 1924 external condition - see also main title page. No.2548 was fitted with long travel valves in 1928, shown by the large casing surrounding the steam pipe on the running plate above the cylinders. The front footsteps were added in the mid-1930s and there are extended brackets on the smokebox door hinges. The latter, along with the smokebox door handle arrangement, was often polished bright. The engine remained attached to a GNR type tender throughout. It was converted to an A3 in 1945 whilst still in wartime black, which it carried from 3/1942 to 12/1946. In due course it became LNER No.49 in 1946 and later, BR No.60049.* (Colour-Rail - Ref: NE2)

ABOVE: *This wintry scene was taken at Marshmoor, south of Hatfield, in January 1939 and shows the original Gresley Class A1 Pacific No.4470* Great Northern *heading a lightweight up express past the signal box and sidings. As GNR No. 1470 this engine had entered traffic in April 1922 and carried GNR livery for approximately 18 months. In this view it carries the standard LNER lined green livery, which it retained until February 1942 when it was painted unlined black. Note the later style non-corridor tender fitted in 1937, replacing a GNR type. No.4470 was never converted to A3 type, being rebuilt by Edward Thompson in 1945 to his own Class A1 design (later A1/1), as a result of which the residual Gresley A1s were re-classified A10. On conversion, No.4470 recieved a royal blue livery lined out in red but from May 1947 reverted to standard post war apple green, now as LNER No.113. The six-car train illustrated here comprises later style Gresley teak open stock, with catering facilities provided by a tourist stock buffet car in green and cream livery. The reporting number seen on the smokebox suggests some form of special working.* (Colour-Rail - Ref: NE1)

BELOW: *Edinburgh Waverley in August 1939 and Class A3 No.2747* Coronach *departs at 10.03am by the North British Hotel clock in the distance - always kept a couple of minutes 'fast' to ensure that passengers did not miss the trains! A K3 Class lurks in the background as the train itself, the up 'Thames-Forth Express' for St Pancras gets on its way. It is destined for a lengthy trip in time terms, for it will travel over the ECML for the first few miles of its journey before taking the Waverley route for Carlisle at Portobello East Junction. South from Carlisle, where the A3 hands over to LMS motive power, the express follows the Midland route, initially over the Settle & Carlisle line. The LMS stock is headed by a yeast van for Burton on Trent which will be detached at Nottingham. In the early 1930s, No.2747 had taken part in the smoke deflecting experiments, which continued on No.2751* Humorist. *Although it is an A3, shown by the superheater header cover on the smokebox, No.2747 carries a round dome boiler. It later became LNER No.93, BR 60093.* (Pendragon Collection - Ref: NE106)

ABOVE: *This superb portrait view, taken in September 1937, shows Class A3 4-6-2 No.2599* Book Law *in ex works condition at Doncaster. This view shows the fine 3/16in red lining applied around frames and axle boxes to particular advantage, also the polished steel cylinder end covers. Note too the black buffer shanks with red lines, along with the black and white lining around the bufferbeam. The top of the tender front plate inside the cab appears to be lined green.* Book Law *was built as an A3 in 1930 and this view shows it in original configuration. When the locomotive reappeared in green again after the war it was renumbered 88 and attached to a GNR type tender - ie with coal rails - which it acquired in 1943. The higher sided modern tenders were more suited to the lines of these handsome locomotives.* (Philip Colebourn Collection)

BELOW: *This second fine Class A3 portrait shows No.2582* Sir Hugo *standing at Grantham in August 1946. This excellent bright shot shows the green livery and especially the red lining almost to perfection; the red lining down the cylinder covers was not always applied.* Sir Hugo *was built in 1924 by NBL Co. and fitted with both vacuum and Westinghouse brakes when new and rebuilt from Class A1 in December 1941. This picture was taken just after the engine was released from a general repair on 17th August, during which it was repainted green and received a banjo dome boiler. It was the first of the class restored to green livery after the war and still carried the older type shaded insignia - the standard LNER post-1946 insignia was Gill Sans style. By October 20th the engine had been given the post war number 83 and was one of only two engines painted in post-war green which ran briefly with their old numbers. It does not carry its home depot allocation, Heaton, on the left hand side of the buffer beam. Note the loaded LMS iron ore wagons running through the station. The station buildings and fittings display a unkempt air, no doubt due to lack of maintenance during the war.* (C.C.B.Herbert Collection, NRM - Ref: NE87)

BELOW: *The design of Gresley's V2 2-6-2s was closely linked with that of the pacifics, combining an A3 style boiler with cylinder and valve proportions whose efficiency was more akin to that of the A4s. Regrettably, few Class V2s seem to have been photographed in colour during LNER days and this view is the only representative in this book of a class which earned the description 'the engines that won the war' amongst many of the LNER staff, given their prodigious feats of haulage on the East Coast Main Line at that time. No.4884, seen near Hatfield in August 1946, was constructed at Darlington during the Second World War in June 1940 and despite its building date, originally appeared in lined green livery; after November 1941 all engines were painted plain black. This scene shows the locomotive recently out-shopped in plain black with LNER restored in full to the tender. It is in charge of an up goods train, typical of the period and with a very high proportion of open wagons. No.4884 was renumbered to 913 in December 1946. The extreme outer lines on this six-track section were used for Dunstable and Hertford branch trains, which parted company with the main line at Welwyn Garden City.* (Eric Bruton - Ref: NE103)

RIGHT, ABOVE:: *LNER 4-6-0 No.5195 was of Great Central railway origin and the first type to carry the B1 LNER Class designation (changed to B18 on the advent of the new Thompson B1 class in 1942). It was one of two engines built to Robinson's design in 1903-4 (Class 8C on the GCR) alongside two very similar 4-4-2s (Class 8B), the idea being to compare them before building large numbers of either. In the event, the GCR built rather more express 4-4-2s than 4-6-0s to this general outline and some of these will be covered later; but No.5195 and its sister engine 5196 did form the basis for a slightly modified batch of ten new 4-6-0s in 1906. These were the more well known 'Imminghams' (LNER Class B4 - see next picture). In this view, No.5195 shows off its attractive proportions at Neasden in 1937. Although but two in number, the original B1s had a long and active life in many different parts of the old GC system and were not withdrawn until the very end of the LNER period, December 1947.* (Philip Colebourn Collection)

RIGHT, BELOW: *In this view, Class B4 4-6-0 No.1482* Immingham *itself stands on Ardsley shed on 23rd April 1949. The design (GCR Class 8F) was a modified version of No.5195 (above) and though* Immingham *was not the first to be built, it gave its name to the class. It was also the only member of the class to receive post war green livery which was applied with the new standard Gill Sans characters. Note the route availability number RA5 just to the right of the builder's plate on the cabside. The lining out on the tender is particularly interesting - see also the previous view of No.5195. Gorton followed a different pattern of lining out on tenders. Each face was treated as a separate panel, thus a rectangle of black with a white line inside enclosed each face, with a further panel of white, black, white lining inside this. Note also the rounded corners to the outer panel. No.1482 was the last member of the class to be withdrawn in November 1950 after some 44 years service. It did not receive its allocated BR number. One hopes No.1482's duties will not be too arduous given the quality of the coal in the tender!* (Pendragon Collection - Ref: NE93)

LEFT, ABOVE: *It is a curious fact that while many railways went from inside cylinders to outside, Robinson's GCR was a little different. After the 'Imminghams' came a batch of inside cylinder 4-6-0s in 1912-13 (the 'Sir Sam Fays' - LNER Class B2, later B19) which were not wildly successful and these were followed in 1917 by a new four-cylinder loco-motive* Lord Faringdon, *GCR Class 9P, LNER Class B3. In 1920, five more of this type were built, one of which was named* Valour *as a GCR war memorial. It became LNER No.6165, seen here pausing at Aylesbury with an up stopping train in December 1938. The special nameplate forms an integral part of the brass beading on the splasher with the black and white lining following its edge. Note also the red lining on the motion bracket and step. The reversing rod is painted apple green and not polished. This side-on view shows the GCR style tender lining once again, notice that the green coal guard is painted black on the beading but without white lining. The engine appears well cared for and polished, excepting the cab roof. Although not very clear in this view, the wheels are lined green. The platform furniture is painted a mid green colour.* Valour *formed part of the Remembrance Day service at Gorton until withdrawal in December 1947.* (Philip Colebourn Collection)

LEFT, BELOW: *Robinson's four-cylinder 4-6-0s had all the ruggedness of construction associated with this celebrated designer but were never as successful as his earlier ones had been nor, in the event, did they enjoy as long a life. In the mid-1920s the class had worked on East Coast Pullman services, but they were not very successful and returned to the GC section in 1927, their work on the East Coast being taken over by the superheated GN large Atlantics. Eventually, in 1929, Class B3 No.6168* Lord Stuart of Wortley *was rebuilt by Gresley using Caprotti valve gear in an effort to improve the disappointing performance. Four out of the six members of the class were altered and Neasden based No.6168 is seen here leaving Aylesbury on 14th December 1938 on ordinary passenger train duty; the lead-ing coach is a vintage low roof GCR brake third from about the turn of the century and a couple of typical pre-war private owner wagons can be seen in the sidings. The B3 loco-motives put up their best performances on the newspaper trains out of Marylebone in the small hours, but more modern Gresley designs were taking precedence by 1938 on the prin-cipal GCR main line services.* (Pendragon Collection - Ref: NE110)

BELOW: *By contrast with the GCR exam-ples, the GER 4-6-0s were relatively small engines - 'ten wheeled 4-4-0s' is no bad description of them! But they were a very succesful type, responding well to Gresley's post-grouping ministrations, and some of them were successfully transferred to Scotland. In this excep-tionally fine view, No.1543, built by Beardmores in 1920 and classified B12 by the LNER, stands at Kittybrewster c.1947, having moved to the Great North of Scotland section in January 1939. It retains the GER Belpaire boiler configu-ration but the slotted GER coupling rod valancing and the brass beading on the cabside have been removed, the latter necessitated by the transfer of the num-ber from tender to cabside from 1929 onwards. The tender is still painted in GER style with black coal guards. Other members of the class in Scotland had this section painted green and lined black and white (c.f. earlier views of GCR 4-6-0s). The wheel rims and tyres are painted green with lining on the outer edge; nor-mally the white line ran just below the spokes, with most of the rim and tyre black. Although repainted in green after the war the locomotive sports older style shaded transfers, rather than plain Gill Sans, with its post-1946 number; it had been LNER No.8543. The red lining has only been retouched below the running plate.* (J.M.Jarvis - Ref: NE35)

ABOVE: *Gresley's LNER was not a particularly wealthy company and although he is quite rightly associated with many famous designs, he was also responsible for the keeping in service (often by rebuilding) of many older types, including some of the 4-6-0s already pictured. However, the situation on the GE section in the 1920s was critical, something more powerful than a B12 was wanted and the Class B17 'Sandringham' 4-6-0 was the outcome, typically Gresley in appearance but, if truth be told, mainly a product of the N.B.Loco.Co. which built the first of them. The first 48 examples were given GER style tenders to keep them within turntable dimensions. In this picture, in order to take a moving train with very slow early colour film, the photographer has succesfuly panned No.2833 Kimbolton Castle as it heads up the GNR main line at Brookmans Park with an unidentified express in 1937. The locomotive was built at Darlington in May 1931 and in keeping with that particular works' practice would have had its cylinders originally painted with a green panel, altered to black at its first repair. Although fitted with a short GER style tender, No.2833 actually worked out of Doncaster during the mid 1930s, along with two other members of the class. They were replaced by Class V2 2-6-2s in 1938 and No.2833 migrated to Cambridge. As BR No.61633, Kimbolton Castle ended its days at March shed, being withdrawn in September 1959.* (K.H.Leech - Ref: NE61)

OPPOSITE, ABOVE: *In more recent years, the B12s were best known in their Gresley rebuilt state with enlarged round topped boiler as seen in this crisp view of newly rebuilt B12/3 No.8537 posing at Broxbourne in June 1939. No.8537 was rebuilt in April 1939 and saw another 18 years service in modified form. The red painted motion and inside frames are visible under the boiler. The locomotive and tender guard irons are also bright red, a variation often applied to GER engines, green or black. Although the tender framing is lined out in red, the ends of the axle boxes have not been lined. The black and white lining on the tender is also interesting, with a large black border and rounded corners. All the class were painted black during the war and only one B12/3 was restored to green with Gill Sans characters afterwards. Note the red oxide fitted van behind the locomotive, painted with small 4in high 'NE' lettering, a style adopted in 1937.* (Pendragon Collection - Ref: NE112)

OPPOSITE, BELOW:*Another view of a Scottish B12 at Kittybrewster in August 1947 shows No. 1524, rebuilt with a modern small round top boiler (Diagram 25A) in September 1946 to prevent it going over the restricted axle load on the GNSR section. The nine examples so treated were reclassified B12/4 in 1948. The B12s had been sent to Scotland in the first instance because of their excellent power to axle load ratio but the Scottish area could not accept the heavier B12/3 rebuild with its larger round top boiler so the smaller boilered rebuild was devised instead. No.1524 has Gill Sans characters, although the tender lettering appears very bold by comparison with most engines which received this new style - a local variant perhaps? Note the polished reversing rod and lack of side feed to the boiler. The Westinghouse pump is black.* (J.M.Jarvis - Ref: NE83)

ABOVE: *New Class B17s built from 1936, were given larger LNER group standard tenders and classified B17/4 in consequence. They also introduced 'Football Club' names replacing the previous 'Country House' theme. Many went to the GCR section and in this view, No.2865* Leicester City, *appropriately based at Leicester shed, heads the 8.20am Manchester (London Road) - Marylebone express at Aylesbury in December 1938. It was built by R. Stephenson & Co. in January 1937 and went new to Sheffield, where it spent its first year before moving to Leicester. By the end of 1938 there were eleven B17s at Leicester. The photograph shows just how handsome a train of teak stock could look. All visible coaches are of Gresley design. The leading coach is a composite brake with 4x3rd class and 2x1st class compartments. The next two vehicles provide catering facilities, Third Class being served by a full open diner without kitchen, second in the rake, meals being prepared in the kitchen part of the 1st class Restaurant Car (Diagram 144), third in the rake. Three of the latter vehicles were allocated to the GC section, Nos.51776/7/8 built between 1931-4. In order to reach the dining vehicles, most passengers would have to trek through a long guard's compartment in vehicle four, possibly because the dining set plus brake composite were added at an intermediate location.* (Colour-Rail Ref: NE12)

OPPOSITE, ABOVE: *The most numerous design of LNER 4-6-0 was the Thompson Class B1 which, although not introduced until 1942, became very widespread from 1946 when bulk building began, continuing well into BR days in 1950. Approximately two thirds of the class saw LNER ownership and since most dated from late 1946 onwards, were certainly the largest class of green engines at the time - but see also the next caption. This splendid view shows Gateshead based No.1100 standing in Newcastle Central Platform 14 with the 4.20pm service for Carlisle in August 1947. The express is due in Carlisle around 6.08pm. The B1s were built in many places but the N.B.Loco.Co. was the main source of supply. No.1100 was one such - the diamond makers plate can just be seen behind the lamp on the left. On the bufferbeam, old style shaded numbers have been used for the engine number. Below this the post 1943 configuration of engine classification and depot identity are placed either side of the drawhook in white paint and in the background of the view can be seen the LNER dark blue enamel station signs with white characters.* (H.N.James - Ref: NE7)

OPPOSITE, BELOW: *Another N.B.Loco.Co. B1 4-6-0, No.1134, makes a fine sight as it stands on Elgin depot in 1948. The class was delivered from 1942-50 and consequently received a number of different liveries when new. The first appeared in 1942 and was given plain black with 'NE' on the tender; only ten were built during the war. Post war deliveries began in 1946 with NBL producing Nos.1040-1093 in lined black livery. From November 1946 until Nationalisation all Darlington built engines and the rest of the NBL order from No.1094 were outshopped in post war green with Gill Sans lettering. No.1134 entered traffic in March 1947. The red lined panel on the cylinders is unique to the NBL engines, Darlington and Vulcan Foundry (the other two builders in LNER times) adopting green cylinder covers. B1s first appeared on the GNSR section in 1946 and worked Aberdeen and Elgin passenger services and fish traffic.* (J.M.Jarvis - Ref: NE33)

OPPOSITE, ABOVE: *It is hard to think of a more suitable way to introduce the 'Atlantic' or 4-4-2 wheel arrangement to this review than with this superb portrait shot of one of the most handsome examples of the genre: LNER Class C4 No.5262 in lined black livery at Leicester Shed, April 1938. These were the famous 'Jersey Lilies' of the Great Central Railway, so nicknamed in honour of a well-known local lady of somewhat ill repute who lived near the locomotives works at Gorton. More prosaically, they were the GCR Class 8B of which the first two were built in 1903 for comparison with the GCR Class B1/B18 4-6-0s considered earlier. As already mentioned, the 4-4-2 type found more favour on the GCR than Robinson's contemporary 4-6-0s and eventually some 27 examples were put into service, surviving intact as a class until 1938 and being reduced by only seven examples at the time of Nationalisation. The example shown here is one of the final Gorton-built batch of 1906. It became LNER No.2920 under the 1946 scheme and was withdrawn early in 1948 without receiving its allotted BR number.* (The late J.P.Mullett - Ref: NE64)

OPPOSITE, BELOW: *The domination of the Great Central Atlantics over the southern end of the GCR main line had come to an end by 1938 when the first withdrawals of the C4 class began - see previous caption - and Class B17 4-6-0s had taken over many of the more arduous duties. However, this view shows that Leicester based Atlantics, seen here in the shape of Class C4 No.5194, could still be called upon to work express services. The engine is the second of the two original examples, Beyer-Peacock built in 1903, and is seen heading a Bradford-Marylebone service at Aylesbury in December 1938; note the LMS Brake Composite (probably a through coach emanating from former Lancashire and Yorkshire territory) at the head of the train. The locomotive, like that in the previous view, is painted in the 1928 (and subsequent) lined black livery and this is slightly surprising. Until 1928, all LNER 4-4-2s received the green livery and after that time, all remained so, save for the ex-GCR and small boilered Great Northern 4-4-2s, 'reduced in rank', so to speak, for no apparent reason! No.5194 became LNER No.2901 in 1946 and was one of the final survivors until November 1950; like all ex-GCR Atlantics, it never received its allocated BR number.* (Pendragon Collection - Ref: NE121)

BELOW: *The North Eastern Railway was an even bigger user of the 4-4-2 type than the GCR but the survival rate of the engines was not as good, almost all being scrapped before BR days. Three types were built of which the pick of the bunch were undoubtedly the fifty handsome three cylinder Z Class Atlantics built to the design of Vincent Raven - LNER Class C7. The first twenty locomotives were completed by the North British Loco Co. in 1911. No.2164, illustrated here at York in August 1937, was built at Darlington in 1914. It was one of only a few which came under national ownership in 1948 (now as LNER No.2970) and was the last member of the class withdrawn, in December of that year. The apple green livery has certain North Eastern touches. The front portion of the frames is lined green, which stops rather abruptly before the splashers. The cylinders are also painted green, another Darlington tradition. Note the lined out ends of the sandwich bufferbeam. The green and cream liveried tourist stock carriage in the background is open brake third No.22270 of 1934.* (Philip Colebourn Collection)

ABOVE: *The Scottish contribution to the LNER Atlantic fleet arose in consequence of the difficult North British Railway routes out of Edinburgh, which were the main reason for the introduction in 1906 of Reid's Class H Atlantics as an attempt to offer something more 'puissant' than the hitherto ubiquitous 4-4-0s. The 4-4-2 wheel arrangement was preferred to the 4-6-0 because of the sharp curves encountered on the Aberdeen and Carlisle roads. Twenty were built to start with, fourteen in 1906 and six more in 1911, all using saturated steam. Superheating of the first batch took place between 1915 and 1921 in which year two new engines were added to the total, superheated from the outset. The six remaining saturated engines were then reclassified I by the NBR. As such they came to the LNER and were classified C10 (saturated) and C11 (superheated). The LNER soon converted the six C10s to C11 form but the 22 strong class remained intact only until the end of 1932; all had gone by the end of 1939. It is thus highly fortuitous that No.9875 Midlothian was photographed at St Margarets shed in colour during August 1939 only three months away from withdrawal. As can be seen, it retained the green livery after 1928, unlike the longer lasting GCR Atlantics already considered. It was fortunate to be the last survivor as it had been withdrawn in December 1937 and subsequently reinstated in June 1938; onset of war prevented its planned preservation. The NBR had issued a series of most resounding names to these noble looking engines which LNER perpetuated in the NBR manner by applying the name to the splasher using shaded gilt letters.* (Philip Colebourn Collection)

OPPOSITE, ABOVE: *The LNER was by far the largest British user of the 4-4-2 type (a wheel arrangement which in tender form was never built after the grouping) and it is not unreasonable to postulate that of all the many types inherited, those of the Great Northern Railway were the most significant, bridging the gap between the dainty Victorian era and the Gresley pacifics. All the GNR 4-4-2s were designed by Henry Ivatt who wisely started with a small boilered version - presumably to get the crews used to the idea before he went further! They became LNER Class C2 and in this view, what was destined to be the last 'in service' survivor of the series, No.3252, basks in the sunshine at Hitchin in 1937, the same year in which the pioneer No.990* Henry Oakley *(LNER No.3990), had been withdrawn for preservation. No.3252 was withdrawn from Retford in July 1945. The 'Klondykes', as they were known (an allusion to the gold rush at the time they were first built) were attractive machines and although originally painted lined green by the LNER the class were, like the GCR 4-4-2s and for similar unexplained reason, demoted to the secondary lined black livery as seen here from 1928; it certainly did nothing for their appearance. The smaller pattern 7½in numerals were needed when the number moved to the cabside as there was very little space on the traditional spartan GNR cab. Note the glass sight screen fitted in front of the cab cut out.* (Philip Colebourn Collection)

OPPOSITE, BELOW: *In the same year as the previous view, Ivatt large boilered 4-4-2 No.3286 stands at Hitchin shed resplendent in pristine apple green livery. The larger size of engine was almost certainly what Ivatt had in mind when he introduced the 4-4-2 in 1898 and the large boilered successors (built from 1902) certainly looked more impressive than their smaller sisters; strangely they were given the same classification by the GNR but the LNER split them logically, the larger version becoming Class C1. Built with a much larger boiler coupled to a wide firebox, they did not reveal their true potential until fitted with superheaters and much of their best work was performed in LNER days after superheating, many examples being on record of performances which would not have shamed a Gresley 4-6-2. No. 3286 was so fitted in 1924, but retained its balanced slide valves. Note that the red lining out on the frames is not continued over the cylinders, themselves lined with a single red line at each end. Although it is difficult to be absolutely sure, it appears that the handrails are painted; but the smokebox door fittings are polished metal. No.3286 became 2815 in January 1947 and was withdrawn in the autumn of the same year. The GNR 4-4-0 behind carries lined black livery.* (Philip Colebourn Collection)

OPPOSITE, ABOVE: *This lovely atmospheric picture at King's Cross in 1939 is yet another fine example of the 'oil painting' quality of some of these pioneering colour images. It shows LNER Class C1 No.3274 leaving (old) Platform 15, behind which was the connecting line from the Metropolitan widened lines. By now, the C1s had been, to some extent, relegated from principal main line duty, though they still had a few 'shots in their locker' as World War II was quite often to reveal. In this view, the 4-4-2 is seen in charge of an ordinary passenger train whose leading coaches (a twin articulated 'lavatory composite plus brake third' pairing) are clearly not of an inner suburban nature and it is probable that the train was a Cambridge service (mid-morning from the angle of the sun), stopping at most intermediate locations. This was, apparently, a common working for the Ivatt engines at that time. It is also possible that it was taken on a Sunday, the presence of the flagman indicating some form of 'line occupation' for essential maintenance.* (Philip Colebourn Collection)

This second successive atmospheric view was taken north of Hatfield in May 1940 and gives a wonderful evocation of a scene which could hardly have changed for many years. Large GN Atlantic No.4434 heads down the main line with a King's Cross to Peterborough stopping train. It is overtaking an N2 0-6-2T No.4725 with a stopping train for the Luton and Dunstable branch. Between the two trains is the down slow line, the whole sequence of running lines being repeated in the up direction beyond the Atlantic. It is interesting to note that the larger train consists of a pair of the notorious articulated 'Quad-Art' sets, so named because they consisted of four coach bodies mounted on five bogies so as to save both length and weight. They had very spartan sized compartments, were none too easy in riding terms and while they may and did serve very well for high density short distance suburban work, one wonders whether they were quite the right sort of provision for an outer suburban service which, with stops, might take some two hours or more to reach Peterborough - but then: 'Don't you know, there's a war on'! The other train is a pair of articulated 'twins'. For the record, the N2s were not officially allowed beyond Welwyn Garden City as they were too heavy for the branch, so why it is on this train is not at all clear! (Colour-Rail - Ref: NE32)

This third example in an attractive trio of 'period' views shows a nice collection of seaside excursion trains lined up in the late afternoon sun at Scarborough in August 1938 and also forms a nice link between the LNER 4-4-2s and 4-4-0s; not to mention a goods 0-6-0 as bonus. As black liveried Class J39 0-6-0 No. 1537, only some six months old, propels stock back towards the station, to the right can be seen the original Class C7 North Eastern Atlantic No.706, whose style of painting shows that there is no such thing as a standard livery; the rear splasher of this green locomotive is painted black with red lining! The screw reverse lever, which replaced steam reverse in April 1935, is visible above the splashers. Last in line is LNER Class D49/2 4-4-0 No.258 The Cattistock, one of the 'Hunt' series fitted with rotary cam operated Lentz poppet valves. Both D49 and J39 were standard Gresley designs, based on Darlington practice, and shared the same boiler type; the D49/2 displays its Darlington pedigree with the green painted cylinders. The visible coaching stock is nearly all non-corridor in type and of entirely NER origin with both elliptical and clerestory roof varieties in evidence. Note the dark grey ash ballast, a form of track treatment which, though well known in pre-group days, lasted much longer after 1922 than is often supposed. (Pendragon Collection - Ref: NE132)

OPPOSITE, ABOVE: *The LNER inherited a fine selection of 4-4-0s from its constituents - and built a few of its own as well - and this review starts with two examples from what is usually known as the 'Scottish School' of design. This was an approach traceable back to William Stroudley and Dugald Drummond who, in their time, served a number of different railways. But very regularly, their successors carried on in the same line of evolution. On the LNER system, the NBR was the main exemplar of this approach and Reid's 6ft 6in J Class 4-4-0, featured here, was typical. Designed with working non-stop expresses over the Waverley route to Carlisle in mind, they had large capacity tenders carrying 7 tons of coal and 4235 gallons of water. No.9900 was the last of the first batch of six, built by N.B.Loco. Co. in 1909. A further 10 examples were built at Cowlairs in 1911. They all carried names associated with Sir Walter Scott's novels and were thus given the soubriquet 'Scott' class. The LNER placed them into class D29 and added superheaters between 1925-36. The NBR had also built some superheated 'Scotts' from 1912, but they had other differences too and these became LNER Class D30. In this view, Haymarket allocated D29 No.9900* The Fair Maid *was photographed at St Margarets shed in August 1938. By now the class was mainly confined to stopping train services, specials and piloting, and allotted the lined black livery - not that there is much, if any evidence of lining in this view. The hand painted name follows the curve of the coupling rod splasher. As will also be seen in the next two pictures, it was Cowlairs practice to use the smaller lettering on the tender.* (L.Hanson - Ref: NE47)

OPPOSITE, BELOW: *LNER Class D34 was the post-grouping designation for the superheated NBR K Class 4-4-0s, a development of a 6ft driving wheel type first introduced in 1909 in saturated form (LNER D33). The D34s were the final Reid design of 6ft 4-4-0 and the two types had the same relationship to each other as the D29/D30 engines already covered. Here, No.9035* Glen Gloy *stands over an ash pit at Eastfield shed in August 1939. The 32 members of the class were built between 1913 and 1920 and the majority worked out of Eastfield shed for many years. Unlike their saturated predecessors they all carried names, Scottish glens forming the inspiration, and they were also known as the 'Glen' Class. Most names came from glens close to the West Highland line, a route with which these rugged 4-4-0s were particularly associated, often working in pairs on heavier trains. However, with the arrival of modern 4-6-0s in the late 1940s and early 1950s they were soon short of work. In 1953* Glen Gloy, *as BR No.62493, was one of eight Eastfield D34s sent work the GNSR section out of Kittybrewster shed. It remained allocated there until withdrawal in June 1960. Under LNER ownership the engines were painted apple green until 1928, when lined black livery replaced it. There does not appear to be any double red lining on the firebox of No.9035. In the background can be seen a departmental tool van, converted from an old NBR six-wheel passenger full brake.* (Colour-Rail - Ref: NE17)

BELOW: *As stated earlier in relation to 4-6-0s, the LNER CME, Nigel Gresley was often willing to continue with developing pre-group designs from other railways, provided the design was sound. Robinson's GCR 'Improved Director' class was such a design and instead of developing a design of his own when new engines were needed on the NB section, Gresley had 24 additional Directors built for service in Scotland. Classified D11/2 (the original GCR machines were D11/1), the new engines were basically the GCR design with cut down boiler mountings and cab to suit the restricted Scottish loading gauge. In this picture, No.6394* Lord James of Douglas *takes water on St Margarets shed in August 1938. When originally built by Armstrong Whitworth in 1924 the locomotive appeared in LNER lined green. However, in 1928 this was changed to lined black as an economy measure. The Scottish works, including Cowlairs, continued to use smaller 7èin letters on the tender sides, as when the locomotive number was also placed on the tender, underneath 'LNER'. The number moved to the cabside and remained 12in. In true NBR tradition, the names adopted for the 'Scottish Directors', chosen soon after the engines were built and again a resonantly Scottish collection, were always hand painted on the splashers. After the war it was announced that all LNER engines were to be painted apple green, with the exception of the A4 Pacifics. Cowlairs was particularly keen on this policy and sixteen D11/2s received this livery including* Lord James of Douglas *now renumbered 2687. The lettering and numbers were applied in plain Gill Sans characters. Note the cleaner patch round the number of the adjacent K3 No.1368.* (L.Hanson - Ref: NE46)

BELOW: *The Great Northern was not the most significant provider of 4-4-0s to the LNER and all appeared during the Ivatt regime. Although depletion was steady through the later LNER period, many remained in service and in September 1944, GNR Class D3 4-4-0 No.4075 (dating from 1897) entered Doncaster works in black livery. Whilst in the works it was selected to haul Officers' special trains and in consequence, was rebuilt with a side window cab and repainted in apple green - at a time when plain black was the general order of the day. On the tender it carried the Company's Coat of Arms, one of only two locomotives to do so; the other was No.4472 for the Wembley Exhibition of 1924. It was also renumbered initially to No.1 but this was soon altered to No.2000. In a rather pointless economy the lettering on the tender was the abreviated 'NE'. In October 1947 this was altered to LNER in full, applied in unshaded Gill Sans characters as illustrated here at Grantham in 1948. No.2000 received its new BR number 62000 in January 1950 together with a cast iron smokebox door numberplate and the BR emblem on the tender; the livery remained apple green. The engine was withdrawn in October 1951 having led a rather idle existence.* (J.M.Jarvis - Ref: NE36)

OPPOSITE, ABOVE: *The GER was a considerable user of 4-4-0s and its designs continued to be developed and improved until 1933. Most of the types (LNER Classes D14 to D16) were from the well known 'Claud Hamilton' family and it is these which will be covered in the next few pictures. In this first view, Class D15/2 No.8891 is seen receiving attention on Bishop's Stortford 'shed' in 1938. No.8891 was one of the first 'Clauds' to be built and came to the LNER in D15, later D15/1 form (ie with small superheated belpaire boiler replacing the original saturated round-top). It was further rebuilt with extended smokebox in 1932 (D15/2) and acquired a GNR pattern chimney in 1936. When this fine view was taken, the engine must have been newly repainted, except possibly for the wheels and frames; splashes of red paint can be seen on the front of the tender. It also seems that there is only a single red line at each end of the boiler barrel. Bishop's Stortford depot was a primitive affair with staff accomodation provided by a grounded coach body and a wooden platform coaling stage. The wagon in the background is on the turntable and displays the pre 1937 style of lettering.* (Pendragon Collection - Ref: NE 125)

OPPOSITE, BELOW: *This second crisp view at Bishop's Stortford in 1938 shows another smart D15/2 No.8893, reversing light engine through the staggered platforms. This engine was received by the LNER in original round-top form and classified D14 at Grouping, but by the time this picture was taken it had twice been rebuilt: in 1926 to D15 (later D15/1) with superheated belpaire boiler and again in 1931 to Class D15/2 carrying a superheated belpaire boiler with extended smokebox. The majority of GER 4-4-0s were given lined black livery from 1928 - excepting the 'Royal Claud' engines (see next picture) and Claud Hamilton itself. No.8893 is also attached to a watercart tender and although it still has its decorative valance there is no red lining around the slots. As in the last view, removal of the original cab side beading and the relocation of the small oval numberplate to the leading splasher has permitted full size cabside numerals to be used. The coaches in the background are part of a Quad-Art set, note the 'Smoking', 'No smoking' and 'Ladies Only' signs on the compartment windows, left.* (Pendragon Collection - Ref: NE 126)

ABOVE: *The D16 (later D16/1) classification appeared just after the Grouping and was reserved for those 'Clauds' rebuilt with larger belpaire boilers closely resembling that of the B12 4-6-0s. As with the GCR 4-4-0s, the LNER also added new engines to the class (ten in number) and these entered service in D16 form. Later, as with the D15s, extended smokeboxes were fitted (Class D16/2) and No.8787 is shown in this form here. This was one of the ten new engines in 1923 and, along with its sister, No.8783, was kept in green livery after 1928 in order to work the Royal Train between King's Cross and Wolferton, for which purpose they were often given freshly painted white cab roofs - an old GER custom. As a result they were generally known as 'Royal Clauds'. The picture shows the engine (with dark roof) at Welwyn Garden City in 1937 in charge of a Cambridge Buffet Car express whose first four coaches are of GNR origin. The engine was rebuilt to D16/3 form (see next view) in 1944, retaining its pierced valances and becoming No.2618 in 1946. Both 'Royal Clauds' ran for a time in LNER green livery with BR markings during the period when they acted as standby to the main Royal engine, Class B2 (rebuilt from B17) 4-6-0 No.61671* Royal Sovereign, *but eventually they went into BR lined black.* (Philip Colebourn Collection)

BELOW: *Apart from the 'Royal Clauds', the only other GER 4-4-0 to receive apple green after the 1928 economies was the original* Claud Hamilton *itself, LNER No. 8900. The engine is on display here at an LNER stock exhibition at Romford in 1936 in rebuilt D16/3 form, a Thompson inspired idea which Gresley endorsed and applied to very many ex-GER 4-4-0s. Claud Hamilton itself was rebuilt to Class D16/3 in 1933 as only the second locomotive to be rebuilt with round top boiler and new cab. However, unlike the first rebuild, it was also given new cylinders with modern piston valves. Following its withdrawal in May 1947 the nameplates were transferred to No.2546 in August. This engine carried the name until withdrawn in June 1957. Note, in this view, the painted not polished handrails and the neatly lined out tool box on the tender (by contrast with No.8787). The decorative valance and brass work has also vanished.* (Pendragon Collection - Ref: NE128)

In this sparkling picture, taken at Cambridge in 1939, No.8835 is newly ex-shops as a D16/3. This conversion involved a new large round-topped boiler of a type first introduced in 1933 - see previous view. It was the final change to the 'Clauds' and the condition in which the majority could be seen at the ends of their lives. In this form, the engines were much more in the 'visibly Gresley' idiom, but their GE tenders and, where retained, their decorative pierced valances, gave the game away; No.8835 was one which lost the decorative valances. It began life in saturated D15 form in 1908, was superheated to D15/1 in 1925 and to D15/2 (extended smokebox) in 1929. It went straight from that form (represented by the previous pictures of 8891/3) to D16/3 unlike a number of its sister engines which went through the intermediate D16/1 and D16/2 'large belpaire' phases. (Philip Colebourn Collection)

The North Eastern Railway had a number of 4-4-0 classes at the Grouping but the only significantly long-lasting type was Wilson Worsdell's handsome R Class (LNER Class D20) which survived intact as a group until 1943 by which time, only two other NER 4-4-0 types remained at all and then only in penny numbers. The 60 Class Rs, dating from 1899-1907 and all built at Gateshead, were highly successful engines, first on the main line and increasingly, in LNER days, on intermediate services. On this work they were gradually supplemented by new Gresley D49s but never rendered wholly redundant until the first DMU period of the 1950s. In this attractive picture, No.1207 (a 1907-built example) is seen 'resting' between duties at Pickering in August 1938. The lined black livery (not unlike that which the NER had used on its goods engines) 'sits' well on the engine and the polished brass splasher beading gives clear evidence of continued pride on the part of the crew at No.1207's home shed, York. The engine would perform two round trips a day between York and Pickering via Gilling. As there was just enough space below the rear splasher beading for the large figures this was not usually removed as it was on the GER 4-4-0s. The curious dotted effect of the lining out is caused by the original Dufay film. The engine became No.2386 in 1946 (BR No.62386 later) and was withdrawn from Selby shed in October 1956. (Philip Colebourn Collection)

ABOVE: *York based D49/2 No.269 The Cleveland slows for the fireman to collect a tablet as it enters the station at Kirkby Moorside, on the single track branch between Pickering and Gilling in August 1937. The line opened throughout in 1875 and was worked by engines from Pickering, a sub shed of Malton, and York. Trains from Pickering usually ran through to York via Gilling and the East Coast Main Line from Bishophouse Junction. In the 1937 summer timetable the afternoon service from Pickering departed at 4.02 pm; the direction of light would suggest that this is the working. The service stopped short of York at Alne arriving at 5.11 pm. Passenger services between York and Pickering ceased from 2nd February 1953 with goods services following suit in August 1964. The engine (built in 1932 and trailing a 'flared top' LNER standard tender) became No.2743 in 1946, while the two-coach train is formed by NER clerestory stock in 'teak' paint. Note the ramp behind the signal box to the coal drops, a typical feature, present at nearly all NER stations, large or small.* (Colour-Rail - Ref: NE18)

OPPOSITE, ABOVE: *The only new design of 4-4-0 to emerge in LNER days was the Gresley D49, conceived in the mid-1920s for intermediate duties in the former NER and NBR areas to replace older pre-group types scheduled for withdrawal. They were the first new design of LNER passenger locomotive and fairly typical Gresley three-cylinder engines, though Darlington built them all and had a free hand with the detailed design. Two main types were introduced, the first series with piston valves (D49/1) and the later series with rotary cam poppet valves (D49/2). They were named either after Counties (English and Scottish, usually with the 'shire' suffix) or Hunts and eventually, the Shire (D49/1) and Hunt (D49/2) names also indicated the class subdivisions (there were six oscillating cam poppet valve Shires for a time - D49/3, later rebuilt to D49/1). Here, Scottish based D49/1 No.2759* Cumberland *stands on the ash pits at Haymarket shed in August 1937. It was built in May 1929 at Darlington with the straight-sided Group Standard tender attached here. In the 1940s, it was involved in two tender changes in which it first received a GCR style tender (1942), later substituted by an ex-NER type in 1947. Note the red lining on the front of the frames and on the fall plate. Two livery details show that although it was based in Scotland between 1932 and 1938 maintenance was carried out at Darlington. The first is the green painted and lined cylinders and the second the low positioning of the number on the cabside.* (L.Hanson - Ref: NE50)

OPPOSITE, BELOW: *In this picture, D49/1 No.2760* Westmorland, *a conventional Walschaerts valve gear engine, reverses out of Glasgow Queen Street (High Level) in 1938 under a fine NBR signal gantry equipped with new LNER upper quadrant signals. The engine carries a red painted NBR style smokebox headboard bearing 'Glasgow' destination. Note the black painted cylinders, indicating a non-Darlington paint job. This and the previously illustrated engine were part of a group of Shires whose first LNER numbers fell into the 2753-60 series. When the 2700-75 series was adopted in 1946 for the whole D49 class,* Cumberland *and* Westmorland *then became Nos.2734-5 and their previous numbers went to Hunts! They were also two of only three Shires not to have the '..shire' suffix; the other was No.2758* Northumberland. *The location is especially unusual for a colour picture at this time; Glasgow Queen Street could be a very gloomy place in steam days. It was the terminus of the original Edinburgh & Glasgow Railway, rail access being down the one-time cable worked Cowlairs Incline. An early traveller described Queen Street as 'in a state little better than the black hole of Calcutta'.* (BR Scottish Region - Ref: NE85)

81

ABOVE: *This view at Mallaig in 1936 offers an attractive reminder of the period when former GNR Class H3 2-6-0s (LNER Class K2) had taken over the bulk of the heavy workings on the old NBR West Highland Line, having been sent north mainly for this purpose. No.4691 was one of 14 members of the class so transferred (to Eastfield shed) in 1925. Six more were transferred in 1932-3 and more still after World War II (mostly in BR days). The K2 was a successful two-cylinder Gresley GNR design developed from his pioneering H2 type (LNER Class K1), of which there were ten, all eventually rebuilt to K2. Eventually there were 75 K2s all told (including rebuilt K1s) and No.4691 was delivered from Kitson & Co. in H3(K2) form as GNR No.1691 in July 1921. The LNER fitted side-window cabs to all Scottish K2s (for extra protection) and thirteen of them (those particularly associated with the West Highland) were named after Lochs, No.4691 becoming* Loch Morar *in August 1933, a year or so after it was fitted with a side window cab. Although painted green by the GNR, the LNER decided on a livery of lined black for the K2 class and the red lining on the tender forms one panel round all three faces of the tender. Together with a number of Scottish K2s this locomotive was painted LNER apple green by Cowlairs in May 1948 with British Railways in full on the tender along with its BR number 61781. From October 1949 BR lined black was applied.* (H.N.James - Ref: NE22)

The LNER received a considerable number of 0-6-0s, to which it added over 300 more (Classes J38/J39) and, if truth be told, this whole group is somewhat under-represented in this survey. The NER was a heavy user of the type and it bequeathed some outstanding examples to the LNER, some of which survived well into the BR period. One of the numerically (and physically) smaller types was the Class P (LNER Class J24) see here, which in an enlarged form (Class P1 -LNER Class J25) was rather more numerous and long-lasting. Wilson Worsdell designed the P Class 0-6-0 in succession to his brother Thomas's earlier C Class (LNER J21). They had 6in smaller driving wheels at 4ft 7¼in, simple expansion as compared with the original compound version of the Class C (all the latter were converted to simple at a later stage) and Stephenson as opposed to Joy valve gear. The LNER took over all 70 examples in 1923 and just under half survived into BR stock. No.1956 heads a local freight at Clifton, just north of York station, under an impressive NER signal gantry in 1938. The engine is in plain black, with the almost orange coloured bufferbeam favoured by Darlington. The leading wagons are owned by the LMS, the most interesting feature of which is the leading wagon which is in the newly introduced 1936 'Bauxite' livery, whose exact hue is often debated. If this picture is even half accurate (and the grey wagons suggest it is), it shows the shade to have been a sort of milk chocolate colour rather than the red oxide often presumed. (Colour-Rail - Ref: NE20)

OPPOSITE, BELOW *This rare wartime view of Cambridge was taken on a crisp and bright May morning in 1942. Both the level of activity and the amount of land taken by the railway are striking in today's terms, though not particularly unusual by the standards of the day. Although Cambridge did not present an industrial image to the world in pre-grouping times, four railway companies had goods depots in the town, the GER, GNR, LNWR and Midland. In this scene, Gresley K3 2-6-0 No.2447 arrives from the north with a loaded coal train probably from the GN&GE joint line. The three-cylinder K3s were outstanding performers, if a little on the 'rough riding' side, and undoubtedly highly influential in Gresley's later 4-6-2 developments. The original ten were of GNR origin but the rest of the eventual 193 strong class (including No.2447, later LNER No.1948) were built continuously by the LNER from 1924 to 1937. They were technically 'mixed traffic' but usually seen on freight duty. Meanwhile a GER J67 0-6-0 tank carries out shunting duties in the sidings to the left. Also visible are the station itself, behind the carriages in the middle distance and immediately to its right, the former GER engine shed.* (Colour Rail - Ref: NE29)

The tender engine review of the LNER is concluded by this fine line-up of ex-works repaired locomotives, seen in Darlington Works yard in 1938. On the right is Darlington built 0-8-0 Class Q5/1 No.794 (NER Class T1 - built 11/1911, wdn 2/1948). This was the last of 90 examples to be built to a Wilson Worsdell design, introduced in response to the growing need for heavy mineral engines. Some of them were rebuilt with larger boilers (Class Q5/2) from former Hull & Barnsley Railway 0-8-0s, but No.794 has the original 'small' version. Next is another Darlington product, Class J25 (NER Class P1) 0-6-0 No.2037 (10/1899, wdn 10/1958), an enlarged version of the J24, an example of which is seen next in line in the shape of No.1843 (built 8/1895, wdn 8/1949) - see also previous caption. No.1843 was a product of the earlier NER works at Gateshead whose closure in 1932 must have been a bitter blow to an already depressed area. The works reopened during the Second World War due to pressure of work at Darlington North Road. Last in line is lined black Class K3 2-6-0 No.2465 built by Armstrong Whitworth in June 1936 and withdrawn in February 1962. Darlington Works closed in 1966, towards the end of steam in the North Eastern Region. (Colour-Rail - Ref: NE26)

The larger passenger tank, though widespread in both variety and area of operation, was never especially numerous on the steam railways of Britain until more recent years, when it usually took a 2-6-4 or 2-6-2 wheel arrangement. On the LNER constituents, it took the form of either a 4-6-2 or 4-4-4 arrangement with one type, illustrated here, being a conversion from one to the other. In 1931, Gresley rebuilt one of Vincent Raven's handsome NER Class D 4-4-4Ts (LNER Class H1) to an equally fine looking 4-6-2 arrangement. The new Class A8 proved a success, greater adhesive weight in consequence of six coupled wheels giving it more versatility, and all 45 were converted by 1936. They proved particularly useful on the steeply graded North Yorkshire lines, especially along the coast line via Whitby to Scarborough. No.1525 was originally built in August 1921 and rebuilt as a 4-6-2T in June 1933. It was to give a further 25 years service in modified form before withdrawal in November 1958. The engine is seen here newly overhauled outside Darlington Works in 1939. The bufferbeam and shanks are a very bright vermilion and once again, although the Dufay original has captured the colour very well, the emulsion dots (see introduction) have also been copied, especially in the fine lining. (Philip Colebourn Collection)

In pre-group days, the intermediate sized passenger tank was regularly of the 4-4-2 wheel arrangement, being in effect the tank engine equivalent of the popular and widespread 4-4-0. Prior to 1923, three LNER constituents (GNR, GCR and NBR) had built them in approximately similar numbers, of which the 51 NBR examples (in two classes) marginally outlasted the rest. The earliest of the two NBR types to appear were thirty of the Reid Class M type, later classified C15 by the LNER and built by the the Yorkshire Engine Co. from 1911-3; No.9133 seen here was the last one delivered, in December 1913. The later NBR 4-4-2Ts (NBR Class L, LNER Class C16) were an all but identical superheated version of the C15s and the link betwen the two designs was much as that already considered in the case of Reid's NBR 4-4-0s. No.9133 was photographed a little way off its native heath at Kittybrewster in September 1937. In the right background can be seen four-plank LMS and LNER coal wagons, both in their respective (officially different!) shades of wagon grey, the LNER example (supposedly darker in tone) having the diagonal white stripe denoting an additional unloading door at the left hand end. The engine livery is black lined out in red, with the standard tank engine configuration of shaded 7½in letters and 12in numerals. Most of the class were withdrawn during the 1950s with two examples surviving until April 1960 on the Craigendoran-Arrochar locals. (L.Hanson - Ref: NE44)

BELOW: The LNER added two new large passenger tank classes to its fleet, though the Thompson L1 2-6-4T Class only existed as one prototype example until batch building began in BR days. Far more familiar in LNER days were the Gresley Class V1 2-6-2 passenger tanks of which some 82 emerged from Doncaster between 1930 and 1939. For the record, ten more were built in 1939-40 (also at Doncaster) with higher boiler pressure but no real change in appearance (Class V3), a state to which the majority of the V1s were modified, mostly during BR days. In this nicely posed view, No.451 of the 1938 batch stands on the depot at Bishop's Stortford in 1939; it was one of the earlier conversions to V3 in 1943. The class worked mostly in Scotland and the North East. But in 1938 fifteen engines were allocated to the GE section, including No.451, and fitted with Westinghouse as well as vacuum brakes. When this picture was taken it was still quite new and the lining out is interesting, especially the red line around the wheel rims and centres. The buffer housings are black in Doncaster fashion with a red line around the end. There is also evidence of a red line between the frames below the smokebox. (Colour-Rail - Ref: NE27)

OPPOSITE, ABOVE: *To concentrate on grime laden work-a-day activity outside the roundhouse shed at Hull Dairycoates in 1939 (or any other shed of that ilk for that matter) must be considered very unusual for the colour photographer of the day and has resulted in a rare record, not diminished by the slight scratch on the original film emulsion, for the main subject is Class T1 4-8-0T No.1350 (NER Class X), the first example of a massive 3-cylinder Wilson Worsdell design of which the NER built ten at Gateshead in 1909-10 for working the huge marshalling yards in the North East ports, which were concerned primarily with the export of coal. The 4-8-0 was a very uncommon standard gauge wheel arrangement in Britain and even when it did appear, was solely confined to tank engines. But rare or not (the T1s were the only 4-8-0s on LNER books), the LNER clearly found them to be useful and added a further five Darlington built examples in 1925; apart from two early 1937 withdrawals (both ex-NER examples), they were kept pretty well occupied until the late 1950s, one even lasting until 1961. Behind the T1, by odd coincidence, is the last example to be built of another NER type perpetuated by the LNER, Class B16 4-6-0 No.1385 built in January 1924 to a 1919 design by Vincent Raven (NER Class S3). It was later rebuilt by Thompson to Class B16/3 and it too had a long life - scrapped 1963.* (Pendragon Collection - Ref: NE137)

OPPOSITE, BELOW: *A coalfield workhorse, LNER Class M1 0-6-4T No.6153, stands amid the usual dirt of a steam shed, in this case Tuxford in Nottinghamshire, during August 1938. The example illustrated was the last of a batch of six built by Kitsons of Leeds in 1904 for the grandly titled Lancashire, Derbyshire & East Coast Railway whose main line ran from Chesterfield (Market Place) to Lincoln (Pyewipe Junction). This section opened in 1897 and all thoughts of Lancashire and the East Coast soon evaporated, though it did settle down to become a useful link across the Nottinghamshire coalfield, as new pits were sunk steadily farther east into the concealed coalfields. The 0-6-4T was not a particularly common wheel arrangement in Britain (six leading coupled wheels were seen as unstable by some railways) and these were the only such types inherited by the LNER, until it absorbed the LPTB stock - see Chapter 3. However, the M1 Class, built to haul coal trains, must have been seen as satisfactory because three more were ordered a year before the LD&ECR was bought by the GCR in 1907. Shunting and trip workings were the norm for this class when the picture was taken - once again an unusual and rare subject for a colour camera in those days. The livery is plain black and No.6153 was withdrawn in June 1946; just over a year later the class was extinct.* (Pendragon Collection - Ref: NE135)

ABOVE: *Well over 1000 0-6-0Ts passed to the LNER in 1923 and the company added to these totals. However, just as with the 0-6-0 tender engines, they are not too well represented in this survey for reasons stated in the introduction. Of the inherited fleet, the NER was the largest single provider and some of its designs (already old in 1923) went on to be amongst the relatively few classes which served until the early 1960s. One such was the Class J71, seen here in the form of York station pilot, No.8286, pausing whilst performing its duties at the south end of the station during August 1947. The J71 design (NER Class E) dated from 1886 and was T.W.Worsdell's standard shunting tank. No.8286 dated from 1892 and in May 1947 was repainted green in May 1947, largely because it was engaged in passenger carriage shunting duties in full view of the public. It was the only J71 to be given this special treatment, which BR repeated in 1950 in darker green, and it ran thus until withdrawal in 1952. As shown here, the characters were all painted cream in unshaded Gill Sans face. The curved top to the figure 6 was not strictly to the Eric Gill pattern (as applied to the A4s with Stainless steel numbers) which British Railways later adopted as standard for the 6 and 9 numerals. There were also many smokebox door numberplates with the curved top variety, especially on the Southern Region. Note the details of lining on the bufferboam, with red painted buffer shanks lined black and white at the end. The coach behind is in plain unlined LMS livery with post war style flat top number three.* (H.N.James - Ref: NE21)

OPPOSITE, ABOVE: *The former GER J67 and J69 Class 0-6-0Ts were closely related types with a very complex history, well outside the scope of this survey, but they were a familiar part of the scene until well after the end of the company period. In this delightful view, J67 No.7169 works a very mixed train over the fascinating Kelvedon & Tollesbury branch at Tollesbury in 1938. There were three trains a day each way with extra services on Wednesdays and Saturdays. To give the line its full title the Kelvedon, Tiptree and Tollesbury Pier Light Railway opened in October 1904, reaching Tollesbury Pier on the River Blackwater in 1907. The line through this desolate part of Essex, or characterful depending on your point of view, was completely agricultural, its main user being Wilkin's jam factory at Tiptree. The Great Eastern and its successors worked the line until passenger services ceased in May 1951. Goods services to the jam factory lasted until October 1962. J67s were the regular motive power. No.7169 was a former suburban passenger example with Westinghouse brakes, and condensing gear until July 1936. Note the destination board brackets on the smokebox. The eight-wheel carriage, with open vestibule ends, was transferred from the Wisbech & Upwell tramway when passenger services over that line ceased in 1928. Both coaches are painted in a light red brown, known as 'teak colour' but bearing little resemblance to teak itself.* (Pendragon Collection - Ref: NE133)

OPPOSITE, BELOW: *After the Grouping, many former GER 0-6-0Ts were transferred to other parts of the LNER, including 20 in 1927-8 to Scotland, where they were none too well received! In this view, one of the exiles, Class J69 No.7348 potters about Eastfield shed on 23rd August 1939. Vacuum brake was added and the condensing equipment removed in December 1927, just before its despatch to Scotland. It was already nearly 33 years old, its work in Scotland was not very arduous and it was withdrawn in December 1953, by then No.8523 under the 1946 LNER scheme. In this picture, No.7348 carries plain black livery, relieved, when clean, by red coupling rods. Behind it are a pair of rather fine NBR bracket shunting signals. Note too the breakdown train in the background, also in black livery. On the right is former NBR Class J36 0-6-0 No.9623.* (Pendragon Collection - Ref: NE134)

ABOVE: *A vintage North British 'Pug' from 1891 stands in the dilapidated roundhouse at St Margarets shed in August 1938. These 0-4-0ST locomotives were a standard Neilson & Co. dock shunter design, but only two of the 38 owned by the NBR were built by the firm itself, the rest coming from Cowlairs. The LNER took over 35 of the 0-4-ST engines at Grouping and classified them Y9. For many years No. 10095 was used on the South Leith duties, shunting in Leith docks. It was not withdrawn until March 1953. The engine is in plain black livery and displays only its number, not its ownership. No.10095 is obviously well cared for with red coupling rods and burnished smokebox door fittings - others of the class had a star shape polished around the door handle, a typical Scottish form of embellishment. Note the tall casing around the safety valves to take steam away from the cab front. These small engines were often loaned to local businesses, although during World War Two a pair ventured much further afield reaching Milford Haven.* (L.Hanson - Ref: NE52?)

In September 1925 the LNER, as part of an experiment with Sentinel steam power, purchased its first shunting locomotive from the Sentinel Wagon Works in Shrewsbury. It was numbered 8400 and used for Departmental duties at Lowestoft Harbour, replacing a GER petrol driven machine and becoming the first of the Y1 Class. The class eventually totalled 24 examples and later Y1s had ventilation grills and lower height cabs compared with No.8400. The GER had established an Engineers' yard and sleeper depot at Lowestoft in 1914 and this view shows No. 8400 on duty there in connection with repairs to the sea wall in 1938 and in lined black livery of non-standard style: the lower panels are lined out in double red with the inner line thinner. Note the shunting rope around the lamp irons and the LMS wagon, still in pre-1936 grey but carrying the new standard (small size) company lettering above the number. The Sentinel shunters had a far longer life than the broadly contemporary railcars and most lasted well into the 1950s. No.8400 became LNER No.7772 in 1943, No.8130 in 1947 and was allocated BR No.68130; but it was transferred to service stock as No.37, in which guise it served until withdrawal in 1956. (The late Sydney Perrier, courtesy C.S.Perrier - Ref: NE96)

OPPOSITE, ABOVE: *During the 1930s, the LNER regularly held exhibitions of stock around its territory especially in the Southern Area and this picture of such an event was taken at Romford in June 1936. GER "coffee pot" Y5 0-4-0ST No.7230, dominant in the foreground, was a particular favourite at such events. Built at Stratford in 1903 to a Neilson & Co. design, it was in service stock as Stratford Carriage Works shunter throughout its LNER existence and fitted with steam heat and air brakes in order to test carriages in the Works. The livery is lined black and is obviously something of a one off given both the shape of the locomotive and the nature of its duties; although red coupling rods were occasionally seen on GER engines, it was not normal LNER practice. The six-wheel Camping Coach No. CC14 behind is painted green and cream in similar fashion to the tourist stock, the roof being pale grey. A freshly shopped Class A3 No.2750* Papyrus *stands in the distance. Once again, it is worth commenting on the accuracy of colour achieved by the Dufay original almost 60 years ago, little affected by the red blemishes in the sky.* (Pendragon Collection - Ref: NE138)

OPPOSITE, BELOW: *The LNER was particularly interested in finding ways of running its branch line services, both urban and rural, more cheaply. The company favoured the development of the steam railcar, although with hindsight this proved to be something of a blind alley. Eighty railcars were built to a number of different variants by the Sentinel-Cammell (latterly Metro-Cammell) consortium for the LNER, the majority working in the North Eastern Area. One such was No.2140* Eagle *a six cylinder car (carriage diagram 96) which worked out of Sunderland shed. It was photographed at its home depot in June 1937, wearing the final railcar livery of green and cream, identical in shade to that of the LNER tourist stock. The cream panels were lined with a fine double green line. A wartime livery of dark brown was adopted, but by then many of the Sentinels were being withdrawn. No.2140 succumbed in October 1944 after a working life of less than 16 years.* (The late J.P.Mullett - Ref: NE68)

The variation in colour between panels on teak stock is readily apparent in this view taken at King's Cross in April 1939. The articulated twin looks to have been recently overhauled as both the varnish and lettering appear bright. Note too the white tyres on the wheels, the centres are in 'teak' paint as are the solebars behind the continuous stepboards. Suburban stock was not lined out. The pair are probably Nos.45611/45612 built in 1936 for the GN section, and are being used here on outer suburban work. The nearest coach is a six compartment brake third seating 60 and it is paired with a lavatory composite (compartments comprising 2 third, lavatories, 2 first, lavatories and 3 third) each built on a 55ft.6in. underframe. The layout meant that all the first class passengers had access to a lavatory in this non-corridor set. (The late Sydney Perrier, courtesy C.S.Perrier)

CHAPTER THREE

LONDON TRANSPORT INTERLUDE

Symbolising the origins of the London Transport system in the shape of the steam worked Metropolitan and Metropolitan District Railways, this remarkable survivor, LT 4-4-0 tank No.L45, stands at Neasden LT depot in 1938. These very distinctive engines were used on both the Metropolitan and the District right up to the time of the electrification of the first parts of the two systems, the example shown being originally built in 1866 by Beyer Peacock as Metropolitan Railway No.23. By 1938 it had been considerably altered with a new design of boiler and a covered cab being amongst the more obvious changes. When London Transport took over the Met. in 1933 five of these veteran Beyer Peacock tanks were still in service and were particularly associated with the rural Brill branch. The closure of the line in late 1935 left little work for the survivors and only No.23 remained at the end of 1936. It was renumbered L45 in 1937 and soldiered on for another eleven years. It was in storage for a the whole of the 1950s before it was restored to its 1903 condition c1960/1. It is now preserved in the London Transport Museum at Covent Garden. (Colour Rail Ref: LT1)

The London Passenger Transport Board

The London Passenger Transport Board (LPTB) was set up in 1933, charged with coordinating passenger services around the Capital. It was in effect the London equivalent of the 1923 main line railway grouping and the new LPTB now became responsible for operating all the services on what had hitherto been a number of smaller companies. These fell into two categories, the familiar deep level 'tube' systems (which are not our concern here) and the older 'surface' lines of the Metropolitan and District Railways whose structure gauge was much the same as that of most British main lines. These two companies had started operation with steam locomotives (the 'tubes' were electric from the outset) and in 1933, the Metropolitan Railway was still using some of them.

In fact, the Metropolitan did not fit comfortably within the basic LPTB rcmit. Although starting from quite modest beginnings (still in existence in the shape of the northern 'half' of the London Transport Circle Line along with the Hammersmith and City route), it had always had main line aspirations and in due course, its main line extended far beyond London and deep into the Chiltern hinterland (often nicknamed 'Metroland') and it also had some freight workings and a small fleet of goods wagons. It was thus an uneasy compromise between a pure inner suburban system and a genuine main line operation and its absorption into the LPTB was not easy.

The Metropolitan had always enjoyed a close working relationship with the Great Central Railway, whose main line into Marylebone shared part of its route with the Metropolitan lines. On November 1st 1937, as part of a rationalisation process to resolve the fundamental dilemma, the LNER, in succession to the GCR, took over all the freight traffic and worked the steam hauled passenger trains north of Rickmansworth, the limit of the electrified services since 1925. Given that all the passenger traffic reciepts for the London area were pooled under the 1933 legislation, this was a useful cost cutting exercise.

As a result of this process, all examples of the former Metropolitan's three larger and more modern locomotive classes were sold to the LNER in 1937. These were, in order of age: Class G 0-6-4T (LNER Class M2, introduced 1915); Class H 4-4-4T (LNER Class H2, introduced 1920); Class K 2-6-4T (LNER Class L2, introduced 1925). The quantities were four, eight and six respectively. From this point onwards, the only use which London Transport made of its remaining steam types was for engineering and works shunting duties.

In the short survey which follows, examples of most surviving Metropolitan types are shown at work during the period around and immediately following the transfer of the larger engines to LNER ownership

When London Transport took over from the Metropolitan Railway in 1933 it retained the old dark red steam locomotive livery, which remained virtually unchanged until the end of Metropolitan steam and was even applied to twelve ex-GWR pannier tanks acquired from 1956 onwards. In this view, G Class 0-6-4T No.97 Brill *displays the distinctive livery at Chorley Wood in 1937. These powerful looking machines were built by the Yorkshire Engine Company during the First World War, with No.97 being the last delivery of four, in March 1916. They were designed for mixed traffic use and all four engines were sold to the LNER in November 1937, numbered 6154-57 and classified M2. All were repainted black (unlined) by the LNER. No.97, as No.6157, was withdrawn from Neasden in January 1943, the first of the quartet to be scrapped.* (Philip Colebourn Collection)

The eight handsome Class H 4-4-4Ts were built for the Metropolitan Railway by Kerr, Stuart & Co. in 1920 and 1921 and used as passenger engines for the prestige services out of Baker Street, taking over from electric locomotives at Rickmansworth. Some trains included a Pullman car service. In this view, now in London Transport livery (basically Metropolitan with new marks of ownership - see previous view), Class H No.109 stands at Aylesbury, probably in the summer of 1937 - note the LT lamp sockets. A few months after this picture was taken the engine became LNER owned and received No.6421 in March 1938. Withdrawn in April 1942, it was the first of the class to be scrapped. The lining out is yellow and black. (Colour-Rail - Ref: LT3)

Aylesbury was a key 'out of town' location in the shared London Transport/LNER area of interest, though the joint line originally promoted by the Metropolitan and GCR went a few miles further North West to Quainton Road. This attractive view, taken at Aylesbury in September 1937, nicely symbolises the relationship immediately prior to the LNER purchase of some former Metropolitan locomotives later that year. The principal subject is an up express from Manchester headed, appropriately, by Class B17 4-6-0 No.2854 Sunderland, *the 'Football Club' B17s being especially associated with the GCR route. Equally appropriately, the first carriage is one of the spacious GCR corridors (a brake composite) and in the bay can be seen an excellent example of Metropolitan carriage livery as applied to its orthodox locomotive-hauled compartment stock.* (Philip Colebourn Collection)

ABOVE: I*n November 1937, when the LNER took over the working of the Metropolitan Railway non-electrified lines north of Rickmansworth from London Transport as well as all freight traffic, the Class H 4-4-4 tanks were classified H2 under the LNER system, the correlation of class letter being merely coincidental. In March 1938, Metropolitan No.108 became LNER No.6420 and is seen here shunting at Aylesbury late in December of the same year. The livery is lined black, a sad decline from the rich red formerly carried. The engines were based at Neasden under LNER ownership, until moved away to the Nottinghamshire area in 1941. They were withdrawn between 1942 and 1947. In the up bay normally used by the Metropolitan trains to Baker Street, is LNER Class B3 4-6-0 No.6165* Valour *on an up Marylebone stopping service. The main line signal is off for an up express in the adjacent platform.* (Pendragon Collection - Ref: NE129)

OPPOSITE, ABOVE: *This lovely period piece at Neasden, with schoolboys carefully recording a trio of lined black locomotives, was taken in August 1938. In the foreground is LNER Class H2 4-4-4T No.6422, ex LT No.110. This was the last member of the class delivered in June 1921. Despite its cleanliness, the new lined livery does not really suit these elegant machines. Behind on the turntable is an example of Robinson's last and numerically largest GCR 4-6-0 design, LNER Class B7 No.5469, of which 38 were constructed between 1921 and 1924. As a mixed traffic type the class was painted in lined black throughout the LNER period - also compare the tender lining with the K2 2-6-0 No.4691 at Mallaig (previous chapter). To the rear of No.6422 is a D11 4-4-0 No.5504* Jutland; *as an express passenger design these had been given apple green livery prior to the 1928 economies. All these locomotives were built within eighteen months of each other, but the D11 outlasted the others by over a decade, being withdrawn from Sheffield Darnall as No.62668 in November 1960.* (Pendragon Collection - Ref: NE130)

OPPOSITE, BELOW: *The Metropolitan K Class 2-6-4 tanks were designed for hauling freight and as such were all sold to the LNER under the 1937 agreement. Six locomotives were constructed by Armstrong Whitworth using parts manufactured under the ill fated scheme to provide work for Woolwich Arsenal after WW1; the boilers were provided by Robert Stephenson & Co. They were delivered in 1925, the last steam engines built for the Metropolitan Railway. All engines and parts manufactured at Woolwich were to Maunsell designs and the K's SE&CR/SR ancestry is very distinct. Classified L2 by the LNER, No.114, seen here at Amersham in 1938, did not receive its LNER number, 6161, until November 1938. However, although the loco is still in LT dark red livery, the London Transport markings on the tanks have been largely obliterated.* (Colour-Rail - Ref: LT2)

This opposite side view of K Class 2-6-4T, No.112 (LNER No.6159), taken at Amersham in June 1938, clearly shows the Maunsell style tapered boiler and firebox, with equally typical fittings such as top feed and snifting valves. Note too the sliding shutters fitted around the cabside opening. The engine was renumbered in October 1938 and still carries London Transport identification and the LT classification below the numberplate. No.6159 was withdrawn in 1943, but the class became extinct in October 1948. (Pendragon Collection - Ref: LT138)

In 1897-9, the Metropolitan purchased two Peckett 0-6-0Ts to replace earlier withdrawn locomotives (actually sold out of service) which had been acquired in connection with the development of the then new Neasden depot (opened in 1882). The two Pecketts remained in LT stock after 1937 and London Transport retained what amounted to the old dark red Metropolitan livery for these and indeed all its retained steam fleet. In this view, No.L.53 is seen at Neasden, where it spent all its working life. (Colour-Rail LT4)

London Transport retained a number of older classes for its own departmental use. One such design was the Class E 0-4-4T. The first members of this class were built by the Metropolitan at Neasden in 1896; in all, three examples were built there and a further four by Hawthorn Leslie at the turn of the century and it is two of the latter engines which are shown here. In the first view, No.L47 (Metropolitan No.80) stands outside the new LT steam shed at Neasden in September 1938 while the second shows the opposite side of sister engine No.L48 (Metropolitan No.81) standing in front of the wooden coaling towers of the power station in 1939. A Class F 0-6-2T No.L50 - see next view - stands behind. The new small shed at Neasden was constructed to service the few remaining steam locomotives following the sale of the larger classes in 1937. (Pendragon Collection - Ref: LT133, Philip Colebourn Collection)

99

The Metropolitan Railway purchased four 0-6-2Ts from the Yorkshire Engine Co. in 1901 and gave them the classification F. In this view, again taken in front of the nearby power station which was owned by London Transport, Metropolitan No.93 is seen at Neasden shed in September 1938, now renumbered L52 under the later LT system. Subsequently fitted with Westinghouse brake apparatus, No.93 was withdrawn from service in 1962 and was finally scrapped in 1964, having taken part in the Metropolitan centenary celebrations in 1963. (Pendragon Collection - Ref: LT135)

GREAT WESTERN RAILWAY

Great Western 'hardware' was almost always instantly recognisable and in this fine study outside Birmingham Snow Hill station on 20th February 1939, a good sample is 'on parade'. Dominant is the typical 'Churchward' shape of 'Saint' Class 4-6-0 No.2937 Clevedon Court *backing out of the station. It displays the fairly short-lived 'shirt button' tender emblem and is well cleaned, but the green livery has photographed 'dark' - not unusual for what was, after all, a very deep and rich colour; but the lining can clearly be seen. As with the red engines of the LMS (Chapter 1), the angle and direction of the sun can make a difference and in this shot, there is an interesting tonal difference between the shade on the vertical flat surfaces of the tender and that on the boiler.*

In the background, as well as the very fine 'three doll' signal, there is a variety of typical GWR rolling stock. Part-obscured by the engine is a short 'Siphon' (GWR telegraphic code name for a milk van), while next to it is a highly characteristic gas cylinder wagon, used for replenishing the gas supply of the many gas-lit coaches which were still to be seen on our railways at the time. Where possible, coaches were recharged at the carriage sidings, but many larger stations usually had at least one gas tank wagon on hand, usually located at the inner end of a terminal platform for easy access in case of emergency. This one is most likely to be empty, awaiting return to the nearest railway gas plant. There then comes a familiar 'Toad' (telegraphic code name for a goods brake van), still carrying the large style lettering which all the British companies abandoned after 1936 in the search for further economy when company goods vehicles were repainted. Finally there is a non-corridor set of steel panelled stock, the GWR being the first British company to adopt this form of external treatment as a 'standard' practice. (Pendragon Collection - Ref: GW64)

An Introduction to the GWR

The Great Western Railway was different from the other three Groups, largely because, unlike them, it did not have to come to terms with the problems of uniting a number of often similar sized railways, each with its own way of doing things; what is more, it did not even change its name. Since the pre-1923 GWR was vastly bigger than any of the smaller (mostly Welsh) railways which came into the group, the new company simply retained the name of by far its most dominant constituent and the GWR, larger than ever, simply carried on much as before; it was never a marriage of equals!

The Great Western was third in size after 1922 and its territory formed an approximate wedge shape with apex at Paddington and extremities located at Penzance in the far South West and Pwllheli (ex-Cambrian Railways) in the Lleyn peninsula of North Wales. There was a penetrating GWR arm into LNWR territory by way of Wrexham and Chester (on its own lines), extending to Birkenhead (for Liverpool), jointly owned with the LMS. The rest of North Wales (including the whole of the north coast) was firmly in LMS (ex-LNWR) hands.

Of the several Welsh railways which came into the GWR Group, that which had most claim to true regional status was the Cambrian Railways (and never forget the 's'!), whose lines filled much of Central Wales and the Welsh border, though not all of it and rarely exclusively. Montgomery, Radnor and Brecknock were the Cambrian heartland with a lengthy cross-country route via Machynlleth to the west coast, dividing at Dovey Junction for Aberystwyth and (via Barmouth) Pwllheli. In South Wales, the pre-1922 GWR already had a strong presence and it shared territory with a number of small, independent and mainly coal-carrying systems, chief of which were the Barry, Taff Vale and Rhymney Railways, all three of which helped fill almost every north-south valley in South Wales with at least one route and often one on each side of the valley. After 1922, all these Welsh companies were absorbed into the new GWR, though 'swallowed up' might be a more appropriate word. There was never a true and equal amalgamation as was usually the case (or at least, meant to be) in the other three big companies.

Within the main 'wedge' and outside the complexities of Central and South Wales (where the LMS also had a competing presence by way of LNWR and Midland interests), and with one major exception, the GWR had the rest of the territory more or less to itself, save at the edges. The exception was where the LMS, in succession to the Midland, cut right across the GWR by way of its own line from Birmingham to Bristol and Bath whence, via its stake in the the Somerset and Dorset, it reached the south coast. The only other significant north-south route across 'GWR country' was the Midland and South Western Junction Railway between Cheltenham and Andover, and it came into the GWR system after 1922.

Along the edges of its bailiwick, the GWR was in competition with the LMS (mostly ex-LNWR) to the north and the Southern (ex-LSWR) to the south. Both relationships were traditionally uneasy, made more complicated by penetrating lines, not to mention that at Exeter, the GWR and SR 'changed sides', the GWR serving the southern coasts of Devon and Cornwall and the SR the north coasts. In the light of subsequent railway history, there can be little doubt who got the better bargain: save for a number of smaller branches, most of the old GWR system remains intact west of Exeter, including five of the larger branches.

The fact that the pre-1923 GWR dominated the new group meant that it also gained another advantage, that of continuity, both in popular perception and in terms of engineering. There was never the remotest possibility that anything other than traditional Swindon practice would prevail after 1922, nor would it have made much objective sense. The GWR engineering tradition was excellent and locomotive, carriage and wagon evolution went on without change, most engines from the constituents which were not quickly scrapped being very soon rebuilt with Swindon style boilers and fittings. Likewise with carriages and wagons: anything other than 'GWR Standard' was allowed to run its course and was then scrapped; there was never, so far as is known, any real attempt to find out if constituent company stock had anything to offer by way of design innovation and in

This picture is surely amongst the finest colour images ever taken of the pre-war British railway scene and is all the more remarkable for having been taken as early as October 1935. It shows King Class 4-6-0 No.6018 King Henry VI *at Exeter St. Davids station with the down 'Torbay Express'. The noon departure from Paddington will have maintained a 60mph plus average speed in order to arrive at Exeter on time at 2.50pm. Eight out of the nine coaches carry roof boards and will be going on to Kingswear, while the last is probably a through coach. From the tender markings, the livery appears to be an early example of the 'shirt button' emblem - the detail is indistinct. The red headlamps and the prominent 'double red' route restriction discs on the cab side are also worthy of note.* (D.R.Barber - Ref: GW45).

truth, it probably had not. But even the mighty GWR could not manage without enlarging the excellent works facility of the old Rhymney Railway at Caerphilly!

The GWR, therefore, had 'history' on its side, with all the advantages that this could bring and, especially in publicity terms, it 'milked' this advantage to the full. It was the only system after 1922 which retained the word 'Great' in its title and it did not let others forget the fact - for who but the GWR could have celebrated its 100th anniversary in 1935, only 97 years after it had run its first trains?(!) But by celebrating the incorporation of the company, rather than the first trains, it stole a huge publicity march on the LMS which actually owned the first main line to serve London.

The GWR was a justifiably proud company but it was often inward looking in consequence of what it felt to be its assured position; while to its rivals, it could often seem plain irritating and uncooperative! And this turned out to be its 'Achilles Heel', for while the other companies eventually took advantage of the multiplicity of talent inherited in 1923, the GWR tended to become a bit complacent. Perhaps because it was still more profitable than the others it saw little need for change. However, by the time of nationalisation, which the GWR opposed more strenuously than the rest, both the LMS and LNER had moved ahead in terms of locomotive development (they lagged well behind in the mid-1920s as several locomotive exchanges demonstrated); while the Southern's electrification had wrought a major transformation of that railway in its own area.

All of these facts go some way to explain the nature of the images which follow, for they display a far more consistent visual unity than in any other chapter. By the mid-1930s, the GWR already looked far more 'together' than its rivals and during the next fifteen years this became more pronounced. But there was still variety to be seen and fortunately, though inevitably dominated by the more prestigious locomotives, a good selection has been possible, including some of the best and earliest examples of any to be offered in this book.

The 'Kings', introduced in 1927, were the flagship engines of the GWR and were evolved in direct line from Churchward's original four-cylinder 'Stars' of 1907 via Collett's 'Castles' of 1923, the two Collett designs being little more than progressive enlargements of the original concept. In this second valuable 1935 view, No.6007 King William III is seen hauling a southbound express in Whitnash cutting south of Leamington. It is not quite as clear as the previous view but it does provide a valuable colour record of the anatomy of a mid-1930s Great Western express. The locomotive is in the classic Middle Chrome Green livery with the small circular totem/monogram applied to the tender, whilst the twelve coach train is in chocolate and cream. Ten coaches have roof boards whilst two third class 'swingers' or strengtheners have been added behind the locomotive. The neat meadow-like slopes of the cutting are redolent of the period and it is easy to see why the GWR 'image' was so attractive. (Colour-Rail - Ref: GW1).

One of the 1930 batch of Kings No.6027 King Richard I stands at Weston Super Mare Locking Road excursion station in September 1937. The locomotive is in the 1934 livery with 'shirt button' emblem and note the white headlamps replacing the earlier red. The special double red restriction, again visible on the cab side, applied solely to the Kings due to their high axle loading and meant that their sphere of operation was strictly limited in GWR days to the principal West of England and Birmingham/Wolverhampton routes, Kings were only able to operate on the Weston loop at a severely restricted speed. Behind the engine, the brake third leading the train can be seen to be a Churchward 'Toplight' carriage. (The late Sydney Perrier, courtesy C.S.Perrier - Ref: GW55)

This splendid pair of views taken at Reading in April 1947, show the 8.30am up Plymouth express passing through non-stop but routed via the up main platform in order to slip the rear coach. The special 'slipping distant' signal, on the extreme right of the large gantry seen in the first picture is 'off'. Motive power is provided by Laira based King Class 4-6-0 No.6010 King Charles I, one of twelve Kings allocated to Plymouth at this date. The engine carries the standard post-war livery with company markings in the form of initial letters separated by the GWR heraldic emblem, while apart from the sixth coach (still in wartime brown), the rest of the fifteen coach train carries the familiar chocolate and cream livery displaying the characteristic 'up and down' level of the dividing line between the two colours which the GWR rarely managed to resolve. To the right of the locomotive is branch line auto-trailer No.179 with the luggage compartment windows plated over.

In the second view, the slip coach guard has detached his charge from the express which is now pulling away from the detached portion. The coach itself is a double brake ended composite in post-war livery with GWR 'coat of arms' and twin lining on the darker colour and it will be brought to a stand at the up main platform. It carries the special slip tail lamps to allow signalmen to distinguish it from the main train. On the luggage trolleys to the right a few train spotters note down the essential details. (H.N.James - Ref: GW3, GW4)

The pioneer King Class 4-6-0, No.6000 King George V, *was built at Swindon in June 1927 and is seen here passing through Reading General with a Plymouth-Paddington (7.15am MSO) express in August 1947. As with the previous example, it is painted in the final version of GWR green livery with the company crest placed centrally on the tender and the initials GW placed either side, though there is no sign of lining in this case. The commemorative American bell, which it received when it went on tour to the USA during 1927, has also been restored following its removal during the war. The leading coach is an ancient (even for 1947) clerestory roof brake still in wartime overall brown. The rest of the coaches are so dirty it is not possible to tell which livery they are painted in, though utility brown seems the most likely. In this context, it presents a far less encouraging impression of post-war recovery than does the smart looking train in the previous views. No.6000, like all the Kings, was given a double chimney during BR days (part of a general improvement programme designed to bring the principal GWR express classes more up to date) and is preserved in that configuration as part of the National Collection.* (H.N. James - Ref: GW2)

C.B.Collett's celebrated Castle Class 4-6-0s, introduced in 1923, continued the Churchward tradition established at Swindon since the turn of the century. In all basic essentials they were an enlarged version of the Churchward Stars and quickly established themselves as the most capable express locomotives in the country, not least in exchange trials with Gresley's LNER 4-6-2s (which came off second best) and by showing LMS management that it was better than anything which had come from either Crewe or Derby in terms of working heavy trains to Carlisle - the LMS Royal Scots were the result! In this view, the pioneer No.4073 Caerphilly Castle, *built in August 1923, stands outside Swindon 'A' shop in November 1937. The livery is the 1934 pattern, with the GWR monogram or 'shirt button' totem placed on the tender and looking rather lost as usual on express designs. The cylinder lining is rather more elaborate than that seen hitherto on the Kings. The polished brass and copper capped chimney perfectly complement the deep green colour.* (J.P.Mullet - Ref: GW37)

This second view of a Castle 4-6-0 in ex-works condition at Swindon in June 1937, No.5009 Shrewsbury Castle, *shows the black and orange lining particularly well, including the lining out of the footsteps and tender frames. The reversing rod appears to be black and note the orange line on the firebox following the contour of the rear splasher. No.5009 was built in June 1927 and withdrawn from Swindon shed in October 1960. (NB At this point it might be worth pointing out that although BR adopted the basic Great Western green livery for its express passenger engines, the lining was not identical, most of the black areas being unlined, except for a vertical double orange line at each end of the cylinders. There was no lining on the firebox and the cab was treated differently with a lined panel placed below the cab windows).* (Pendragon Collection - Ref: GW56).

This further quite excellent and rare early view from 1935, scarcely affected by the fact that the very slow early colour film has not quite been able to 'stop' the front end, shows No.5041 Tiverton Castle *as it enters Exeter St. Davids station on a down Plymouth express in early October. The locomotive carries the 1934 livery with 'shirt button' monogram on the tender, while also worthy of note are the red head-lamps. A Toplight brake composite leads the formation and since it is followed by a brake third, the first coach is likely to be a through vehicle, destined to be set out from the train later in its journey. This picture also shows that everything was not always immaculate on the pre-war Great Western - both the station canopy and nearby signal gantry could certainly use a repaint!* (D.R.Barber - Ref: GW46)

In this April 1939 scene at Oxford, a somewhat dusty looking No.5044 Earl of Dunraven *(formerly* Beverston Castle *- see next caption) sets back in order to loosen couplings as it is about to come off the Birkenhead-Bournemouth through train and give way to Southern Railway motive power in the shape of SR 'King Arthur' Class 4-6-0 No.742. A railwayman is in attendance and the Southern continuation will be found in the next chapter. Note that the nameplate does not carry the explanatory words 'Castle Class' below the name itself; in later years this extra embellishment was usual when the name did not include the word 'Castle'. The leading horse boxes are also coming off here and are LMS vehicles, though from where they came is not known. Horses were regarded as valuable traffic by the railways and merited special treatment. They travelled in passenger or 'passenger rated' trains (ie at higher speed than goods trains) and for their conveyance, purpose-built vehicles were provided which contained padded walls, to avoid injury to the horse(s), and a separate small compartment (seen at the near end of each vehicle) for the attendant travelling groom. The railways lost this traffic during the 1950s and 1960s in favour of the roads but it is interesting to note that modern road 'horse box' design owes much to its rail-borne ancestor.* (Colour-Rail - Ref: GW10)

Castle No.5054 Earl of Ducie *passes Reading on the up through line hauling an up express from South Wales (probably Swansea, with through portion from Neyland) during an April afternoon in 1947. The engine is in the post-war GWR green livery and although traces of orange lining can be seen on the boiler and firebox, there is no apparent sign of the elaborate cylinder cover treatment seen in some earlier views. No.5054 was built in June 1936 and was originally named* Lamphey Castle, *receiving its new name in September 1937. The majority of Swindon Lot 303 built in 1936/7 were renamed after Earls in 1937. The leading coach is still in wartime overall brown livery.* (H.N.James - Ref: GW8)

The Castle with a unique number 100 A1 displayed on two cabside plates and named Lloyd's *is seen here at Reading General in April 1947. It started life as Star Class No.4009* Shooting Star *and was converted to a Castle in April 1925, being renamed and renumbered in 1936 - note that the nameplate now carrries the inscription 'Castle Class' below the main name. The Castles and Kings had been painted plain green during the war but the locomotive's livery is now post-war lined green, without any lining out on the black areas. No.100 A1 is shown here fitted up as an oil burner; many locomotives were so fitted during the 1946-7 coal shortage and carried sliding metal shutters on the cab as seen here, but the results did not justify its continuation. The leading luggage van of this express is of Southern origin.* (H.N.James - Ref: GW9

Based at Cardiff Canton, No.5054 Earl of Ducie *is seen again at Severn Tunnel Junction in May 1947, hauling an up South Wales express consisting of the usual mixed collection of carriage styles. A Toplight brake third is at the front while third in the formation is a wide-bodied, centre-kitchen, composite dining car: note the distinctive, so called 'clipper' profile, compared with the rest. It is a flush sided vehicle and possibly one of many which the GWR, in conjunction with the firm Hamptons, had completely refurbished after the war. Locomotive and train are mostly in post-war livery although the second carriage is still in utility wartime brown. A typical GW junction station nameboard can be seen to the right.* (H.N.James - Ref: GW7)

Again from Cardiff Canton, Castle Class 4-6-0 No.5007 Rougemont Castle *glints in the sunshine as it approaches Reading General with the 8.15am up express from Cardiff, due Reading 11.10am, in August 1947. In the background the signal for the up main platform is off, but the slipping distant is at caution as the train is stopping. The leading coach is a 70ft 'Concertina' brake third dating from 1906/7. These coaches were so called because their doors were vertical and set back slightly from the main side panels in order to keep the width within the defined structure gauge. Close observation of the leading end of the vehicle will reveal this fact if the vertical flat doors are compared with the slight inward slope to the roof of the main panelling.* (H.N.James - Ref: GW6)

Churchward's four cylinder Star Class set the pattern for Great Western express passenger locomotives for the rest of the Company's independent existence. A total of 73 was built, including the Abbey Class, between 1906 and 1923; a number were later rebuilt as Castles. In this early view, taken in August 1936, No.4012 Knight of the Thistle, *built in 1908, enters Reading General with a heavy up express. The locomotive has the typically spartan Churchward cab with no side windows and offering limited shelter to the crew, while the engine is attached to the smaller (low sided) 3,500 gallon tender and the whole ensemble carries the pre-1934 livery with 'Great Western' in full, Note also that the upper side sheets of the tender are fully lined out. The difference in colour between the weathered full brake and the clean livery on the second vehicle is also revealing.* (Colour-Rail - Ref: GW12)

This magnificent ensemble of a Star and Castle double heading an up express was taken at Reading in August 1937. Standing in the up relief platform the train is headed by Star Class 4-6-0 No.4020 Knight Commander *which is piloting the well known No.4082* Windsor Castle. *Both locomotives carry the 1934 livery with 'shirt button' monograms, as ever looking somewhat insignificant. This picture also shows that lining was retained on the upper panels of the smaller tenders with the 1934 livery. C.B.Collett's enlargement of the Star Class to produce the Castles is particularly evident in this view; though both types shared what amounted to much the same sort of running gear, the more massive proportions of the Castle are readily apparent. Late on in life a number of a Stars received outside steam pipes similar to the Castles and some late post-war survivors also received the larger pattern tenders, making the differences not quite so obvious.* (Philip Colebourn Collection)

Star Class 4-6-0 No.4014 Knight of the Bath stands *in Shrewsbury station, about to head a train for Birkenhead via Chester in 1938. It is sporting the 1934 livery in not very good condition which, together with the fact that the brass splasher beading has long gone, having been removed during the first world war as with all the Stars illustrated in this survey, endows the whole colour scheme with a slightly drab air in consequence. The engine displays the outside steam pipes and larger tender which give it rather more the appearance of a Castle.* (The late P.B.Whitehouse - Ref: GW28)

Oxford station in April 1939 is the setting for this attractive view of Star No.4021 British Monarch, *still with the original 'front end' configuration and coupled to a small tender, heading an up ordinary passenger train, consisting of a four-coach non-corridor set. Here, compared with the last view, the livery is in much better shape, though one could wish that the brass splasher beading had been reinstated; Great Western green always looked infinitely better when allied with plentiful brightwork. A Hall Class 4-6-0 (No.4988* Bulwell Hall) *stands on the up through road. The Star's red route restriction code is carried high on the cabside.* (Philip Colebourn Collection)

The 1924 rebuild of Churchward two-cylinder 4-6-0 No.2925 Saint Martin *with 6ft driving wheels was the forerunner of Collett's highly successful 4900 Hall Class mixed traffic locomotives, which were built in quantity from 1928 onwards. No.4916* Crumlin Hall *was an early example, built in 1929, with smaller pattern tender. The locomotive is seen at Leamington Spa station in 1935 with an up express and it carries the 1934 style livery. The stock is quite a mixture of old and new: a fairly modern bow-ended corridor third leads, also carrying the monogram, followed by a Dean clerestory composite (which seems to have had a fair amount of its original wood panelling replaced by steel sheeting) and a gangwayed 'Siphon G'. Leamington station was extensively rebuilt in the late 1930s, work commencing in 1936.* (Colour-Rail - Ref: GW15)

The Saint Class, from which the Halls were derived, is illustrated on the title page of this chapter but only Saint Martin *was actually rebuilt with 6ft wheels. The rest of the Halls were built new and here, another 1929 example, No.4921* Eaton Hall, *draws alongside the old up platform of Leamington Spa station in 1935 bearing the reporting number 790 - composed of painted white numbers slotted into a frame - which denoted the Birkenhead to Bournemouth through train of Southern railway stock. The train has a six-coach Maunsell corridor set leading, note the characteristic recessed brake ends, followed by a further six unidentified Southern coaches with one GWR example (a Restaurant Car?) 'cut in' to the formation. The locomotive again carries the 1934 livery and trails the low-sided tender.* (Colour-Rail - Ref: GW24)

The photographer almost left it too late to record this fine impression of Hall Class 4-6-0 No.4917 Crosswood Hall *crossing the river Exe as it leaves Exeter St.Davids station with a down express in October 1935. This engine is paired with an intermediate height tender which, on close examination, can just be seen to be carrying lining on the upper panels - the general state of cleanliness is none too good for what is often regarded as the height of the 'Golden Era' of steam railways. Apart from the leading van and Toplight brake third, the stock cannot be identified. But to compensate, there is a magnificent, almost tree-like bracket signal gantry controlling the entrance to platforms 6, 5 and 4 in the up direction. The two outer distant arms, controlling the diverging tracks from the 'straight ahead' route are fixed and there are calling on arms below all the distants, lettered CO on a red background.* (D.R.Barber - Ref: GW49)

The last example in this unique quartet of views, all showing the same class of engine in one of the earliest years when colour film was available, was again taken at Leamington Spa in 1935, No.4913 Baglan Hall *being the featured engine, this time with a replacement high sided tender and carrying the pre-1934 livery. It is seen entering the station with an up express (reporting No.785), probably for the Southern Railway via Reading. The rather mixed bag of carriages is 100% Great Western. Once again this view shows how quickly the cream upper panels of the coach livery weathered.* (Philip Colebourn Collection)

ABOVE: *The only new 'large passenger' engines designed by the GWR after the Kings were the 30 County Class 4-6-0s, built under Hawksworth's supervision between 1945 and 1947. They had 6ft 3in driving wheels, a new size for the GWR, and giving them mixed traffic capability. There was even mention of a possible Hawksworth 6ft 3in pacific too, but nationalisation was to stop all that. Of notionally equivalent power to a Castle, their smaller driving wheels made them especially suited to the steeply graded lines west of Exeter, as seen here in the shape of a very grimy No.1018* County of Leicester *leaving Teignmouth and heading along the sea wall with the up 'Devonian', the Kingswear to Bradford express, composed of LMS stock. From Bristol, the locomotive would hand over to motive power of LMS type, more than likely a Jubilee 4-6-0. Although it is now June 1949, there is no visible sign of change to the new BR order, hence the inclusion of the picture in this chapter.* (E.D.Bruton - Ref: GW 62)

OPPOSITE, BELOW: *In this view, what is believed to be No.5974* Wallsworth Hall, *and hardly in the pristine condition so fondly imagined by GWR enthusiasts, is seen shunting in Swindon Yard on 5th September 1937. The engine has an intermediate size tender and in front of it are two Locomotive Department coal hoppers in overall grey livery, each with different markings. In 1936 the Big Four companies simplified the lettering style on their wagons, with the company initials, wagon capacity and number now being displayed in small characters in the bottom left hand corner of the wagon side. The new 4in high initials can be seen on No.53081 (left), whilst No.53071 displays the old 16in style. The hoppers themselves were built to handle coal for Swindon works (as here) and for the Park Royal power station in London.* (The late Sydney Perrier, courtesy C.S.Perrier)

The Grange 4-6-0s, introduced in 1936 were essentially Hall Class engines with smaller 5ft 8in coupled wheels which, along with some other parts, were taken off withdrawn Churchward 4300 Class 2-6-0s and reused. No.6832 Brockton Grange, *built in August 1937, is caught here at the north end of Birmingham Snow Hill station on 20th February 1939. Only the top express engines were given lined green livery at that time, the small wheeled Granges appearing in plain green livery with the GWR monogram on the tender, although copper capped chimney and brass safety valve cover and splasher beading provided some decoration. The front of a Toplight carriage can be seen on the extreme right while the gas tank wagon immediately in front of the locomotive is that which is also seen on the title page to this chapter, the two pictures having been taken by the same (unknown) photographer on the same day.* (Pendragon Collection - Ref: GW65)

'Duke' Class 4-4-0 No.3256 Guinevere *brings the style of the Dean era to this April 1939 view taken at Newbury station, enhanced by a double brake ended Dean clerestory composite of similar vintage. The locomotive simmers gently in the down bay platform as it has a long wait before departure with the 12.25pm for Southampton Terminus. No.3256 is in pre-1934 unlined green livery with 'Great Western' on the tender and the carriage has the post-1934 simplified livery with 'shirt button'. Many contemporary observers noted that the GW green could very quickly turn a much darker and bluer shade, especially on less important (unlined) classes, Although early colour film is not always reliable this would appear to be the case in this instance. In the Lambourn Valley Bay on the up side of the station, the unique Diesel railcar No.18 awaits departure with the 11.47am branch service.* (Colour-Rail - Ref: GW16)

The Dukes were an extremely versatile type whose 5ft 7½in driving wheels made them suitable for a wide variety of jobs. Introduced only three years after the abolition of the broad gauge in 1892, they were in a sense one of the first fruits of Dean's 4ft 8½in 'standardisation'. Hardly surprisingly, when larger Belpaire boilers began to be developed at Swindon (from the late Dean period onwards), it was not long before a large boilered version appeared and in due course took its class name, not from the first example but from No.3312 (later 3311) Bulldog which had actually started life as a Duke! Subsequently, while some Dukes were given replacement small boilers with Belpaire boxes (as in the previous picture), others were rebuilt to the larger form, which version was also adopted for widespread new construction. When Churchward arrived on the scene, it was not long before the larger and more powerful Bulldog Class began to display his familiar visual lines, exemplified here by No.3444 Cormorant, *newly ex-works at Swindon in July 1937 carrying the plain green 1934 livery. This was one of the later 'Bird' series of Bulldogs, built new in 1909, well into the Churchward era.* (L.Hanson - Ref: GW31)

It would be inappropriate to cover the full and complicated story of the double framed GWR 4-4-0s in this book (it is well recorded elsewhere) but suffice to say that it did not end until the engine class illustrated here was built, for despite its late Victorian appearance, 4-4-0 No.3215 is in fact of 1937 vintage and one of a 'new' class of 29 engines. Introduced in 1936 using Duke type small Belpaire boilers on Bulldog frames, they were regarded as Duke replacements, though strictly speaking they were rebuilt Bulldogs. Not very surprisingly, they were instantly christened 'Dukedogs'. A series of 'Earl' names was allotted and many ran thus adorned until it was felt inappropriate to use such exalted names on such quaint engines. The 'Earl' names were then transferred to Castles and the new 4-4-0s thereafter ran nameless. They were later renumbered into the 90XX series and became particularly associated with the Cambrian lines. No.3215 was allocated to Didcot during the late 1930s and in this picture is bringing a Southampton local into Worthy Down on the Didcot, Newbury and Southampton line; note the large non-standard front windows. It was withdrawn as No.9015 in 1960. (Pendragon Collection - Ref: GW67)

ABOVE: *The Churchward 43xx 2-6-0s were an early attempt to move forward from the familiar 0-6-0 type to provide a locomotive with greater speed (the leading pony truck gave added stability at higher speeds) and which also offered better mixed traffic capability. Introduced in 1911, they were excellent engines and continued to be built with minor variations right into the 1930s, when well over 200 were in service. Collett's final version, introduced in 1932 and numbered in the 9300-19 series, had side window cabs in place of the spartan Churchward type carried by the older Moguls. In this excellent detail view, No.9303 takes water from the column at the end of the down main platform at Reading in April 1947; it sports unlined green livery with the post-war lettering GWR on the tender. Behind the tender a container is carried in an LMS five-plank open wagon which has only been patch painted in the corner in order to carry its details in the new 'economy' style - a common alternative to full repainting during and after the war. When the new wagon lettering style was adopted in 1936, the LMS introduced brown livery (which it called 'bauxite' and whose exact colour is often debated) in place of the previous grey, and this 'patch' may well be an example of the shade adopted. (H.N.James - Ref: GW23)*

OPPOSITE, ABOVE: *A Churchward 28xx Class 2-8-0, No.2834 of the 1911 batch, trundles through the Whitnash cutting with a heavy goods train c.1935, ten of the wagons being iron ore empties (some Guest, Keen & Baldwins) probably for O.I.C Banbury. The locomotive still displays pre-1934 livery with 'Great Western' in full and has a large pattern chimney. In common with other unlined locomotives both chimney and safety valve cover are painted over. Churchward first introduced the design in the form of No.97 (later 2800) in 1903 as Britain's first 2-8-0 and it proved so outstandingly successful that it remained the standard GWR heavy freight type for the rest of the company's existence, while the Stanier LMS 2-8-0 was in many respects a modern version of this GWR type on which Stanier must have worked when at Swindon. The engines were built in batches over a good many years, perhaps the most surprising thing being that after an interval of almost 20 years (1919-38), construction was resumed under Collett's direction and the class total, was almost doubled - from 84 examples to 167. From 1938 onwards side window cabs were fitted and the last members of the class were built at Swindon in 1942. (Philip Colebourn Collection)*

OPPOSITE, BELOW: *In 1911, J.G.Robinson had introduced a highly successful 2-8-0 for the Great Central Railway which was later adopted as a standard World War I freight type by the Railway Operating Divison of the Royal Engineers, to which end many more were built. They were always referred to as RODs and after the war, many of them. now surplus to Army needs, were sold to the main line companies. The LNER (naturally, being in succession to the GCR) procured many of them while the LMS also acquired a fair number (usually for their tenders only!), but somewhat surprisingly, the GWR also purchased a quantity, which almost certainly delayed the need to build further 28xx 2-8-0s for quite some time (above). In this view, No.3016 enters Leamington Spa station with a down through freight in 1935. It was one of the original batch purchased in 1919 and has 'Great Western' in full on the tender and a GWR pattern safety valve cover, but has retained original chimney and dome. A set of Southern stock, composed of fully lined out Maunsell corridor coaches and forming the Birkenhead to Bournemouth service, can be seen on the up line. (Colour-Rail - Ref: GW17)*

The 'Aberdare' 2-6-0s, introduced by Dean in 1902, were the freight equivalent of the Bulldogs (above) and Churchward's influence in their evolution was clear from an early date. However, by the time this picture was taken in 1937 these double framed engines were already something of an anachronism and withdrawal of the class was by then under way. No.2622 (built in 1901 as the third example of the class) stands at Swindon in newly applied plain green livery with the 'shirt button' monogram applied to its Great Central pattern tender, acquired from one of the ROD 2-8-0s purchased by the GWR after World War I - see last view. These rather imposing looking engines were primarily coal haulers and their name denoted their first useage: Aberdare to Swindon coal trains. The class mostly performed heavy freight duties, in particular mineral haulage, to the end. No.2622 was condemned in 1946 and the twelve examples which entered BR service had all gone by the end of 1949. (L.Hanson - Ref: GW32)

The 'Dean Goods' was an oustanding 19th Century 0-6-0 design which first came into service in 1883, well before the abolition of the broad gauge. Eventually, 280 examples were built down to the end of 1899 and they were seen far and wide on the GWR system. Here, No.2550, in pre 1934 livery, heads light engine along the down through road at Birmingham Snow Hill station in February 1939 - it was a Snow Hill pilot engine at the time. No.2550 was one of 108 Dean Goods taken over by the War Department during 1939/40 and was sent to France as WD No.153, while at the end of the war it went even further afield to China in connection with UN relief activity. A GWR two-cylinder 4-6-0, probably a Hall Class, stands in the up main platform with an up train. Note the simplified livery applied to the toplight coaches. The station itself is little altered from its 1910-12 remodelling. (Philip Colebourn Collection)

Dean Goods 0-6-0 No.2460, built in 1895, stands at its home depot of Severn Tunnel Junction in May 1947. It carries the post war livery for secondary classes, plain green with the letters GWR on the tender, though the green is very dirty; the allocation STJ is placed just behind the bufferbeam. The Dean Goods type had a very light axle loading and was therefore particularly suited to branch line workings. Furthermore, it acquitted itself well against some of the more modern post-war types of comparable power and was even given a 2MT (mixed traffic) power classification by the LMS dominated BR management. No.2460 was one of many which went to BR and was one of the last half dozen or so to survive, being finally condemned in April 1954. (H.N.James - Ref: GW18)

There were never too many locomotive types of non-GWR pre-grouping origin on the GWR at any time after 1922 and certainly not when most of the pictures in this book were taken. However, Ex-Cambrian Railways 0-6-0 No.892 lasted the course and is seen here in charge of an up ordinary passenger train at Harlech in February 1941. Built by Robert Stephenson & Co. in June 1903 as Cambrian Railways No.93 this Jones designed 0-6-0 remained in service until April 1953. By the time of this picture, it had gained some GWR features: most longer term survivors from the absorbed companies received some form of 'Swindonisation'. The livery is overall black, a wartime economy measure. Note the concrete signal post with lower quadrant arms. (Colour-Rail - Ref: GW22)

BELOW: *In 1903 Churchward produced No.99, the prototype for his standard class of large 2-6-2 tank engines with 5ft 8in coupled wheels. It was followed by 39 more in 1905-6 (3111-49), together with 41 broadly similar 3150 series in 1906-8 with larger boilers (3150-90) - see next but one view. When No.99 was renumbered 3100 in 1912, the original version was known as the 3100 Class. In 1928, Collett rebuilt No.3148, with detailed variations, and it became the basis of his own version for new construction from 1929 onwards - the 5101 Class. During the next year or two, the whole of the 3100 Class were similarly rebuilt and then renumbered into the 51xx series, their numbers (5100/5111-49) being intermixed with the new 5101 engines. In this picture, No.5128 (old No.3128) was seen in typical 51xx territory, Leamington Spa, on 5th September 1935. Suburban tanks were not shopped as often as express passenger types, so older styles of livery lasted considerably longer on the more humble engines, as displayed here with No.5128 in pre-1934 plain green. Note the up platform bracket signal with centrally pivoted arms.* (Philip Colebourn Collection)m

OPPOSITE, ABOVE: *The 51xx series of 2-6-2Ts was a somewhat confusing group, containing as it did both rebuilt and renumbered Churchward 3100s (5100 Class) and Collett's new engines, correctly known as the 5101 Class if it was important to differentiate between the two. But the latter could always be distinguished by the fact that they had a curved 'drop' at the front between the upper and lower running plate, as seen here on No.5192, built in 1934 and standing in the up main platform at Leamington Spa with an ordinary passenger train from Birmingham Snow Hill in 1935. The 5101 type was also differentiated at first by the outside steam pipes with which they were built, but later, some of the Churchward engines were modified to this form. The GWR 'shirt button' monogram was first applied during 1934, so No.5192 must have been one of the last new engines to appear with old style lettering. It has the less restricted blue route code and a polished copper cap chimney. The 51xx series remained the backbone of Birmingham area suburban services well into BR days and were finally ousted by the introduction of DMUs.* (Colour-Rail - Ref: GW19).

BELOW: *Churchward's original larger boilered 2-6-2Ts, the 3150 Class of 1906-8 (based on his 3100 Class), were never renumbered in the 51xx series and this broadside portrait of No.3163 (built 1907) shows the pleasingly balanced outline achieved with these engines - note too the vertical 'Churchward' drop between upper and lower running plate. The location is Leamington Spa c.1935 and the locomotive is in charge of an up express (probably semi-fast from Snow Hill) of non-corridor stock. The livery is pre-1934 plain green with Great Western in full on the side tanks; the route restriction colour and power code are on the sliding shutter and the headlamps are still red. Both this locomotive and the rebuilt No.3101 (see next picture) were withdrawn in 1957.* (Philip Colebourn Collection)

Aylesbury station is again the setting for this excellent view, taken in Summer 1938. A train has just arrived on the down island platform with an afternoon service from Princes Risborough via the GWR/GC Joint line. Both locomotive and train are modern GWR suburban types. The 61xx 2-6-2 tanks (see previous view), represented here by No.6106, were still quite new (note that the engine still carries its original livery), whilst the flush-sided, four-coach non-corridor stock was a modern approach to providing the maximum number of seats within the available loading gauge rather than offering too much by way of passenger comfort. The sets contained two third brakes and two composites, the first class compartments (four in each composite, along with five thirds and all in a 57ft length) being in the centre of the set. The station itself was managed by a three company Joint Committee as the main line was operated by the LNER (Great Central) and London Transport (Metropolitan Railway), providing services to Marylebone and Baker Street respectively. (Philip Colebourn Collection)

OPPOSITE, ABOVE: *Another example of the 3150 Class is seen here in 1936, again at Leamington Spa. No.3156 is on an up passenger train, running under express headlamps and probably from Birmingham Snow Hill, comprising a four-coach Birmingham Division set of 70ft non-corridor coaches with a four-wheel van in the rear. The wider spaced first class compartments in the centre of the set can clearly be seen and it is perhaps worth noting that these unusually long coaches (for suburban types) had no fewer than eight compartments in the third brakes and eleven (6T + 5F) in the composites. No.3156 was withdrawn in 1938 but reappeared as a '3100' Class 5ft 3in 2-6-2T No.3101 in 1939, 31xx numbers (see above) having been revived for this new type.* (Colour-Rail -

OPPOSITE, BELOW: *The 6100 Class was a development of the 51xx type for the London suburban area and was given higher boiler pressure. Introduced in 1931, they had the Collett style of front end treatment - see previous captions - and were near-identical in appearance to the earlier 5ft 8in engines. In this view, London Division 61xx 2-6-2T No.6149 performs shunting duties at Aylesbury (Joint) station in October 1938, it carries the 1934 livery with GWR monogram.* (Colour-Rail - Ref: GW20)

OPPOSITE, ABOVE: *As well as its numerous 5ft 8in 2-6-2Ts, the GWR also made use of many smaller 2-6-2Ts with either 4ft 1½in or 4ft 7½in driving wheels. The latter, seen here in the form of No.4539 at Newquay in 1936, were the 4500 Class, developed in 1906 from the smaller wheeled Churchward 4400 Class of 1904. Essentially a branch line type which worked all over the GWR system, the 4500 Class was found especially valuable in the South West where, in Cornwall in particular, the small wheels and modest coupled wheelbase were ideally suited to both the gradients and curvature of the branch lines in the Duchy. The engine shown was one of ten built in 1913, the first to display a curved 'drop' to the front running plate; while the class itself went on building until 1929, no fewer than 120 of them appearing after the Grouping, No.4575 onwards having sloping top tanks and increased weight. No.4539 is not particularly clean (was the GWR of the 1930s always as smart as is often supposed?) and still carries the pre-1934 livery.* (Pendragon Collection -Ref: GW69).

OPPOSITE, BELOW: *Ever expanding coal export traffic from South Wales meant that the GWR required increasingly powerful locomotives to cope with bigger mineral loads. However, the distances covered by these trains (usually in the South Wales valleys) was generally well within the compass of a large tank engine and Churchward first contemplated a 2-8-2T version of his 28xx 2-8-0. Eventually, however, the idea took shape as a 2-8-0T, still based on the 28xx type, the first of which came out in 1910. Eventually, 195 of the 4200 Class 2-8-0 tanks were built down to 1930. Depression in the early 1930s took away much of their work and some 54 of them were rebuilt as 7200 Class 2-8-2Ts from 1934 to 1939 so as to improve their sphere of operation. During the war, the GWR then found itself short of the 2-8-0T version and built ten new 4200s in 1940 to replace an equivalent number of 2-8-2T rebuilds. In this view, 2-8-0T No.4283, dating from 1920 and one of the first to be built with the enlarged bunkers which all eventually displayed, stands outside Swindon works 'A' shop in November 1937 in sparkling condition after a full repaint - plain green with GWR monogram. These engines rarely looked this smart for very long!* (J.P.Mullet - Ref: GW40)

BELOW: *The typical GWR shunting engine was of the 0-6-0 pannier tank arrangement and from mid-Victorian times, hundreds were built down the years to many 'variations on a theme', while many hundreds more had panniers added after they had been in service in a different configuration. Yet not for the first time in this survey, it has to be pointed out that one of the most ubiquitous types of engine has almost escaped coverage by the early colour photographers; however, this one is of more than usual interest. It shows the veteran open cab 2021 Class 0-6-0PT No.2055 blowing off and seemingly impatient to return to work having taken water at Maidenhead in October 1945. The engine was one of many built for the GWR at Wolverhampton Works and dates from January 1899, pannier tanks having been added in 1925. The livery is probably overall black but could be very dirty green and even the water splashed over the tank side fails to reveal any marks of ownership. It was originally built as a saddle tank and was withdrawn from service at Danygraig shed in January 1951.* (H.N.James - Ref: GW43)

ABOVE: *By contrast with the other sections of this book, it has been found possible to complete this chapter with a few, more general views of the old GWR, starting with a rather nice atmospheric shot of Bristol Bath Road shed on 5th September 1937, taken from the platforms of the adjoining Temple Meads station soon after the rebuilding of both. The shed was completely reconstructed using money from the Goverment's Loans & Guarantees Act of 1929, the new buildings being finished in 1934. The coaling stage and repair shop (steel frame with brick infill) are both new, while the shed is out of view to the right.*

The combination of 'against the light' shooting and Dufaycolour has given almost an 'oil painting' quality to the image, not for the first time in this survey. The locomotives identifiable are Saint Class 4-6-0 No.2979 Quentin Durward (left) and Star Class 4-6-0 No.4048 Princess Victoria*, nicely symbolic of the Churchward revolution in both two- and four-cylinder form; both of them are in very fair condition and display the 1934 style livery. It is also worth mentioning that in the 1930s, the original Churchward 4-6-0s were still seen as 'front line' power and the two examples shown were not withdrawn until 1951 and 1953 respectively. In fact, many of the later Halls and Castles (especially those which appeared in BR days) were built to replace rather than supplement the older engines.* (The late Sydney Perrier, courtesy C.S.Perrier - Ref: GW59)

BELOW: *If the last picture has 'oil painting' quality, this rather nice misty winter view of the Regent's Canal (Grand Union) and the GWR main line near Old Oak shed, taken from Scrubs Lane bridge, can perhaps stand for the impressionists; but what a timeless and evocative scene despite the hazy detail - all it needs is a horse drawn narrow boat on the canal! It is more than a little reminiscent of the similar view taken by the same photographer at Willesden (Chapter 1); both were clearly deliberate in spite of the visibility. In this picture, a London Division 61xx 2-6-2T is seen in charge of a down local passenger train comprising a six-coach 'city' set, whilst empty coaching stock from Paddington is nearest the camera. The line climbing in the foreground crosses the main line via the girder bridge in the background and provides a link to the down side of the main line from the shed.* (The late Sydney Perrier, courtesy C.S.Perrier)

Yet another delightfully atmospheric picture by the late Mr Perrier shows a near-deserted Paddington station on a gloomy wet day in the 1930s with the station roof obviously in need of repair! The featured carriage is a Toplight corridor brake third in 1934 livery, marshalled in a Paddington to Birkenhead express with the one time familiar roof boards reading 'Paddington, Birmingham, Shrewsbury, Chester, Birkenhead for Liverpool'. The benches in the foreground are also typical pieces of GWR station furniture and combine with everything else to offer a truly typical picture of the contemporary railway environment; but how many others at the time would have even bothered to look twice? Thankfully, even though the weather prevented the result being of the best quality, this photographer did! (The late Sydney Perrier, courtesy C.S.Perrier)

This fascinating and rare wartime view of Worcester loco shed, a Divisional Headquarters, was taken from Rainbow Hill in September 1942. The coaling stage and three road through shed can be seen in the middle ground, but the other shed building is obscured by trees to the right. The line up of locomotives in the foreground includes a couple of strangers: behind Grange Class 4-6-0 No.6841 Marlas Grange *in 1934 style green livery, comes LNER J25 0-6-0 No.2141, one of forty loaned to the GWR during the war, the majority being allocated to the Worcester and Wolverhampton Divisions; while bringing up the rear is Marsh I3 4-4-2 tank No.2091, one of two (2088/91) loaned to the GWR by the Southern in 1941. An open cab 2021 Class 0-6-0PT shunts wagons immediately behind and a closed cab pannier tank can also be seen. The Oxford, Worcester & Wolverhampton main line curves through the site to the rear of the coaling stage and on the far side of the main lines are the locomotive and carriage works buildings. Two auto trailers can be seen in front of the buildings behind the chocolate and cream coach. The wagons partly hidden by the trees in the foreground are on the line to Worcester Foregate Street station. Most of the visible wooden bodied coal and mineral wagons were once privately owned, but were operated in 'pool' during the war and never returned to private ownership; but two higher capacity GWR loco coal wagons can be seen near the coaling stage.* (Pendragon Collection - Ref: GW74)

This chapter is concluded with a fine view taken deep in the heart of Great Western territory in the Forest of Dean where it had to share an interest in the Severn and Wye system with the LMS (ex-MR). A handsome AEC diesel railcar No.W7 stands at Coleford (Severn & Wye) station in July 1950 with a charter from Birmingham. Although 2½ years into Nationalisation the railcar is still in GWR livery, without company markings and only the W number prefix indicating a change of ownership. Railcar No.7 was introduced in July 1935 with bodywork by Gloucester Railway Carriage and Wagon Co. and was one of a number of railcars for the introduction of which the GWR became justly celebrated. A total of 38 railcars was built for the GWR (the first 18 being 'streamlined', the rest more angular in outline) and there were several subtle variations including two full parcels cars and others designed to run with trailers. In many respects they foreshadowed the BR DMUs and were certainly the most successful pre-BR diesel units. Note the colour scheme of the water crane. (The late P.B.Whitehouse - Ref: GW52).

SOUTHERN RAILWAY

No one image was wholly typical of the Southern Railway, but if one can perhaps exclude the electrified lines, which served millions of commuters, then perhaps the most widespread perception of the railway was that it served so many holiday destinations - older readers will surely recall the famous 'little boy' poster and 'Sunny South Sam'. Allied to the holiday theme, the Southern, for historical reasons, also made more use of Pullman cars than any other of the Big Four and it is the dual holiday/Pullman theme which is represented here, combined with the most celebrated new design of steam locomotive which the Southern introduced, photographed at one of the most famous railway locations in the world, Clapham Junction.

The date was August 1947 and the train is the down 'Devon Belle' Pullman, the last to be introduced of the several Southern Pullman trains which carried the 'Belle' theme, though BR added a few more 'Belle' names later. Instituted in 1947 as an early attempt to revive holiday traffic after the war, the 'Devon Belle' made a most attractive sight in those austerity early post-war days. It soon became very popular, loading to as many as 14 cars at peak times - a proper task indeed for the new 'Merchant Navy' 4-6-2s which had been introduced in 1942 and which regularly took the train as far as Exeter. Here, No.21C11 General Steam Navigation is in charge, displaying what must be said to be a less than normally clean Malachite green livery but with an added splash of colour in the form of the special headboard and side 'wings' used on this service. However, in spite of the size which this train achieved, and its popularity, it was never a major commercial success and the gradual growth in car ownership during early BR days caused it to be killed it off in 1954. (H.N.James - Ref: SR3)

An Introduction to the Southern Railway

The Southern Railway was, by quite some margin, the smallest of the Big Four; but it was equally fascinating; indeed it was probably more complex than any of the others in proportion to its size, a fact reflected in the (slightly greater) length of this introduction compared with the other lines - for the Southern was undoubtedly different, for three principal reasons.

Firstly and from the outset, it pursued an extensive policy of suburban electrification, already started by two of its three main constituents and under active consideration by the third. This meant that steam traction was not the universal prime mover which it remained on the other three groups and that the development of Southern steam power was confined simply to such as was needed in order to work the non-electrified lines. This in turn gave less need to build new steam designs and more incentive to keep the older types fully serviceable until superseded by electric trains. In consequence, proportionally more pre-1922 steam locomotive variety was present for a longer time than on the other systems, an aspect which continued well into BR days.

Secondly, the Southern was different in the sense that it was essentially a passenger railway and the only one of the Big Four to gain the majority of revenue from this form of traffic. In consequence, the domination of passenger types in this chapter is not as untypical as it is elsewhere in this book. What is more, because of its widespread electrification, the SR never built any new locomotive hauled non-corridor stock at all; there was no need. Thirdly, the Southern was a much more 'London orientated' railway whose inner London network (see below) was far more complex than that of the other three.

Nevertheless, it has to be said that this survey is still unbalanced in the sense that it concentrates on the steam side of the Southern. This is because, rather like the less glamorous goods trains, not to mention the plain black engines of the other three railways, the new Southern electrics did not seem to command much attention from the early colour photographers.

Geographically, the Southern possessed a compact system with very little real competition save at its interface with the Great Western for traffic to the far South West (mainly Exeter and beyond), already mentioned in the previous chapter. Furthermore, it only had three principal constituent companies, none of which was overwhelmingly bigger than the others and thus able to dominate the group. Happily, it had both good engineers and good managers who quickly began to integrate the best features of all three constituents to the mutual benefit of the system - which was just as well since the SR did not enjoy the best of reputations in its early days, all three of its constituents being seen by its often critical (and equally often well-heeled and articulate!) outer suburban customers as a little behind the times compared with the rest of the country!

Marginally the largest of the Southern constituents was the London and South Western Railway which, from its original London and Southampton origins, had become the only one of the Southern constituents to enjoy proper 'trunk route' status. Like the GWR, its territory in 1922 formed a wedge shape with apex at Waterloo, its only London terminus. In the west, its main 'terminus' was Plymouth (via Okehampton), plus long extensions to Padstow and Bude (both in North Cornwall) and Ilfracombe (via Barnstaple) in North Devon, the whole of the LSWR west of Exeter often being referred to as 'The Withered Arm'! In the east, its boundary was the route from London, via Guildford to Havant, whence it reached Portsmouth via a short stretch of the London Brighton and South Coast Railway to Portcreek Junction and a joint LSWR/LB&SCR line onwards. The LSWR also had its own alternative route to Portsmouth via Alton, Fareham and Cosham, not to mention the original London and Southampton main line via Basingstoke, later extended to Bournemouth, Poole and Dorchester.

Within LSWR territory, the only competing 'cross' routes were the GWR line (and its branches) from Yeovil to Weymouth and another GWR line from Newbury to Winchester. There was also a SE&CR presence in the Guildford area (below). These apart, the LSWR had a strong territorial monopoly.

Adjacent to the LSWR was the aforementioned LB&SCR, the smallest of the three Southern constituents but a very well known railway none the less. It too occupied a wedge of territory radiating from London, though in this case it had two London termini, Victoria and London Bridge, in each of which locations, its station stood side by side with that of the South Eastern and Chatham system. Quite apart from its main line to Brighton, the LB&SCR also had a circuitous route to Portsmouth via Horsham and Chichester and a direct line to Eastbourne. The 'Brighton triangle' was completed by a lengthy coastal route from Portsmouth to Eastbourne with an extension to St Leonards and Hastings.

The final SR constituent was the South Eastern and Chatham system, a joint operating organisation dating from 1900 which ran the routes of the nominally still independent (and once fiercely competing) South Eastern and London Chatham and Dover railways. By 1922 it was to all intents and purposes a single system with its own livery,

The original Bulleid Merchant Navy Class 4-6-2 No.21C1 Channel Packet *is being checked over at Exmouth Junction shed in June 1949; this would require some care as the class in its original form was particularly temperamental. No.21C1 emerged from Eastleigh works in 1941 and a total of 30 of these large pacifics was built down to 1949, the last batch of ten under BR ownership. The whole class was subsequently rebuilt into a more conventional form in the 1950s. In this view it is still in as built condition with the exception of the smoke deflecting arrangements at the front end of the casing. The livery is Malachite green with three yellow lines along the casing, coupled with a full set of Southern brass number and nameplates applied to both engine and tender. A visit to Eastleigh works in October 1949 brought a much needed repaint, the engine being then turned out in BR standard blue and renumbered into the BR series as No.35001. Rebuilt in August 1959, No.35001 was withdrawn in November 1964.* (The late W.H.G.Boot - Ref: SR15)

engineering design and so forth. However, because of its 'two company' history, it virtually monopolised the lines in Kent. It also made a modest penetration into East Sussex from Tunbridge Wells via Hastings to the Sussex/Kent boundary beyond Rye and owned an East-West route from Tonbrige to Reading, most of it in sole ownership but using running powers over the LSWR through Guildford to link the two independent sections. In SE London, it owned a veritable 'cat's cradle' of lines and had no less than five inner London stations: Victoria, London Bridge, Charing Cross, Holborn Viaduct and Cannon Street. At the first two, it stood side by side with the LB&SCR (above) while it gained access to the latter three via through platforms at London Bridge. Holborn Viaduct was also reached by direct links from Brixton and Herne Hill on the SE&CR route to Victoria.

In spite of this complexity, the lines of all three constituents only met up at one location, Clapham Junction, and even that was mainly LSWR/LB&SCR. But this was a vital nodal point because the Thames formed a barrier to North-South traffic and from Clapham Junction there also ran the vital link across the river to the GWR and LMS (ex-LNWR), the West London Extension, whence travelled much through freight traffic. The main SR link to both the LNER and the LMS (Midland Division) was via Blackfriars and the Metropolitan widened lines while another Southern link to the LNER was the gradient-restricted East London Joint from New Cross via Rotherhithe Tunnel to Shoreditch, where reversal took place.

At the grouping, the inherited steam locomotives retained their original numbers with an appropriate letter prefix to denote origin. But by the time of this survey, the Southern had rationalised the system, LSWR engines retaining their old numbers, while SE&CR and LB&SCR types had 1000 and 2000 respectively added to their old numbers. New SR types took up appropriate gaps, usually in the LSWR allocation, except for Bulleid's own designs which were numbered in a new way, starting with figures to represent the number of axles taken up by the non-driven wheels, followed by a letter denoting the number of driven axles and then a serial number for the individual locomotive in question. Thus 21C denoted a pacific (4-6-2 elsewhere) and C (no carrying axles) was the code for 0-6-0. After nationalisation, BR would have none of this and simply gave the Bulleid engines unused five figure number blocks in the Southern Region 3xxxx series.

Merchant Navy No.21C11 was the first example of the intermediate batch of ten locomotives built between December 1944 and June 1945. It appeared in wartime black livery and was soon named General Steam Navigation. Note the unusual full rounded casing ahead of the cylinders which was unique to this locomotive. After the war this group was also repainted in Malachite green with yellow stripes as seen both here and on the chapter title page. Following No.21C2 all the Southern built Merchant Navies were numbered and lettered with transfers rather than brass plates. Only the cast smokebox door plate was retained, latterly a full circle with building details in the bottom segment, the first engines having originally been fitted with a 'horseshoe' style plate. This view shows the engine about to 'ring off' Nine Elms shed for its next turn of duty in April 1947. It became BR No.35011 in November 1948 and was rebuilt in July 1959; withdrawal followed in February 1966. (H.N.James - Ref: SR20)

This particularly clear view of Merchant Navy Class pacific No.21C12 United States Line was also taken at Nine Elms, its home depot, in April 1947. The side of the casing is all Malachite green, with a thin strip of green above the top yellow line on the locomotive only, while in order to maintain a straight line at the green/black divide, the upper edge of the smoke deflector is painted black. The lettering is rendered in post-war sunshine style, with black shading on the Malachite areas and Malachite shading above the bufferbeam and note (compare previous view) that the smokebox plate is now painted red. As BR No.35012, this engine was withdrawn from Nine Elms in April 1967 following some ten years service in rebuilt form. (H.N.James - Ref: SR1)

Merchant Navy No.21C18 British India Line *charges through Raynes Park with a down Weymouth express, Nine Elms duty No.54, in September 1946. The engine is in Malachite green but the visible Maunsell carriage stock, with the possible exception of the second vehicle, is still painted dark olive green. It was by no means unusual to see the darker green pre-Bulleid carriage livery at this time and indeed, there is a contemporary report in the Railway Observer of 1948 to the effect that dark green coaches were still being revarnished with their new BR markings; presumably if the paintwork was sound, this was a sensible economy measure. The bushes on the left completely disguise the urban character of the surroundings and it should also be commented that it was remarkably rare for anyone to try to capture a 'full speed' train in colour at that time.* (E.D.Bruton - Ref: SR57)

OPPOSITE, ABOVE: *The down 'Devon Belle' approaches Basingstoke hauled by Merchant Navy No 21C13* Blue Funnel *in September 1947, towards the end of its first season of operation - see also chapter title page. Initially this Pullman service operated three days a week, Friday to Sunday from Waterloo and Saturday to Monday from Plymouth and Ilfracombe. Here, No.21C13 sports the post war Malachite livery together with an eye catching set of nameboards, a typically bold example of Southern publicity. The train has at least thirteen cars and just visible at the rear is the special 'Devon Belle' Pullman observation car, introduced for this service. Merchant Navies generally handled the train east of Exeter, with their lighter cousins the West Country Class taking over the western sections. Regrettably, no Southern Railway vintage colour views of the latter type have been located, though the 'lightweight' 4-6-2s do feature in Chapter 6.* (H.N.James - Ref: SR4)

OPPOSITE, BELOW: *The 'Bournemouth Belle', introduced well before the war and reinstated in 1946, was a far more established and commercially viable sort of Pullman operation than the post-war 'Devon Belle' - and it well outlasted the newer service too, not being finally withdrawn until 1967. Here, the umber and cream cars of the down train pass through Basingstoke station in September 1947, headed by Merchant Navy class 4-6-2 No.21C19* French Line CGT, *in the standard post-war Malachite green. The rather badly proportioned headboard is painted to match the locomotive's livery. The typical Southern platform furniture is also worthy of note, including the green and white nameboards and standard concrete lamp-posts. Judging by the wheelbarrows, sleepers and ballast, track maintenance work is in progress.* (H.N.James - Ref: SR5)

BELOW: *Before World War II, the sixteen Lord Nelson Class 4-6-0s were the largest locomotives built by the Southern; unfortunately their performance did not always match their size. It was not until Bulleid fitted Lemaitre multiple-jet exhaust coupled with a large diameter chimney to the engines that this Maunsell four-cylinder design finally rid itself of steaming problems. Taken on a dull day, this close up view of No.864* Sir Martin Frobisher, *seen at Waterloo in July 1939 about to depart with a West of England express, shows the newly fitted chimney as well as the freshly applied Bulleid livery. In the late 1930s the new CME, Bulleid, tried a number of shades of green coupled with a more modern bold style of lettering before settling on the Malachite shade displayed here. Note the mainly green smoke deflectors and the sanded and burnished buffers. Only six members of the LN Class were operating on the Western Section (ex-LSWR) at this time, the other ten being employed on the Eastern Section (formerly SE&CR) Continental boat train traffic, but the coming of war quickly changed all that.* (The late Sydney Perrier, courtesy C.S.Perrier - Ref: SR49)

LSWR Class N15 4-6-0 No.747 Elaine *heads an up express at Exeter Central in August 1936. No.747 was built to a Robert Urie design of 1919 which was to be the basis of Maunsell's own developed version for the Southern in 1925. For publicity reasons, Southern management asked Maunsell to name these engines and it was an inspiring thought to use names drawn from the legends of King Arthur and his Knights, many of whose exploits allegedly occurred in the territory served by the Southern. Thereafter, whether pre- or post-group in origin, they were always known as 'King Arthurs'. In this picture, the leading coach is one of the handsome but not very numerous wooden panelled ex-LSWR 57ft corridor types, followed by fully lined Maunsell corridor stock, whose characteristics were, for the most part, derived from the final steel panelled LSWR type, the LSWR having been the only major user of corridor stock (Pullmans excepted) amongst the three Southern constituents. The paintwork on the leading coach seems rather faded by comparison with the later vehicles; this is most likely to be caused by weathering of the livery.* (Philip Colebourn Collection)

Urie King Arthur Class 4-6-0 No.739 King Leodegrance *pauses at Winchester with the 11.30am Waterloo to Bournemouth express in Summer 1938. As in the previous view, the locomotive is paired with a bogie tender to LSWR design, another idea which was also adopted by Maunsell in SR days. Both locomotive and train are in the standard Maunsell dark green livery. The leading coaches, four-car set No.204, are Maunsell pattern corridors dating from 1930 and still fully lined out - a detail just visible on the original transparency - and the whole ensemble is in superb external condition. During this period, a Dining Car set was usual on the Waterloo-Bournemouth services and one such appears to be 'cut in' to the centre of the train. The engine was finally withdrawn as BR No.30739 from Bournemouth shed in May 1957.* (Colour-Rail - Ref: SR6)

Yet another 'Urie Arthur', No.742 Camelot, *features in this fine view taken at Oxford in April 1939. In continuation of an operation whose earlier stages (with GWR Castle No.5044* Earl of Dunraven) *were seen in the previous chapter, it has just backed onto the carriages of the Birkenhead to Bournemouth through train which comprises a mixture of Southern and Great Western stock. The locomotive is in Maunsell dark green livery with black and white lining; note the black smoke deflectors. In June 1939 it was repainted in lighter olive green with Bulleid style lining and lettering. Wartime conditions eventually brought the drab overall black livery to the class, No.742 being the first to succumb, in June 1942.* (Colour-Rail - Ref: SR7).

The Maunsell version of the King Arthur Class 4-6-0 was introduced in 1925, ten being built at Eastleigh, officially as rebuilds of Drummond 4-6-0s, and thirty more by the North British Locomotive Co. Eastleigh contributed a final batch of fourteen in 1926/7. A readily distinguishing feature of these 'Southern Arthurs' was the continuous curve between cab side and roof, well seen in this superb rear end view of No.789 Sir Guy *(one of the NBL series) on an up express at Templecombe in 1939. It carries the relatively short-lived Bulleid experimental light olive green applied to a number of Southern passenger locomotives in the late 1930s. Insignia are now repositioned and rendered to a new Bulleid style in a rather pale shade by comparison with the richer 'old gold' colour of the Maunsell insignia. The view is unique in giving a definitive impression of the pre-war Bulleid style of unshaded tender lettering, rather weak in character compared with the so-called 'sunshine' style which replaced it after the war - see next but one picture (and others). The lining out on the other hand is in the Maunsell tradition of black and white with areas such as the coal guards and smoke deflectors finished in plain black; but note how the former reflect the green shade to give almost a deep green appearance. Templecombe station was rebuilt in the late 1930s and the extended platforms have been constructed in Exmouth Junction concrete.* (The late S.C.Townroe - Ref: SR30)

No.774 Sir Gaheris *was one of the NBL series which were often, unsurprisingly, also referred to as '"Scotch" Arthurs' or simply 'Scotchmen' (not 'Scots' be it noted!) and indeed, with Urie's influence via the original N15 design plus the NBL Co., these engines were very much in the Scottish tradition. This April 1947 view shows the engine in post-war Malachite green livery standing in Nine Elms shed, fortunately for the photographer under the hole in the roof where a bomb fell in 1940. The livery seen was applied in November 1946 and during the early war years, it ran in Bulleid light olive green. There are some very obvious changes compared with the previous view - green wheels, green smoke deflectors and the, now yellow, lining taken to the top of the tender coal guards, for example. But the cylinders covers remain black. Unfortunately, it is not always possible, even in a colour picture, to determine the colour of some areas which quickly became weathered or dirty, doubly unfortunate in the case of Southern green liveries, which were never wholly consistent in either colour or lining at any time during the period covered by this survey.* (H.N.James - Ref: SR22)

This last King Arthur picture returns to the Urie LSWR version in the form of a fine rear 3/4 portrait of No.740 Merlin *at Eastleigh early in 1948. A number of interesting details may be noted: the large tank in the tender coal space shows it is an oil burner, one of five members of the class so fitted in 1946/7 (by the end of October 1948 it was a coal burner once again) and electric lamps are visible on the smokebox top and above the smoke deflector, the equipment having been fitted to this engine in early 1948. The livery is Malachite green, though it looks very different in hue from most of the Malachite coloured engines in this review. Likewise, it is alleged to be lined black and yellow, though it looks black and white. However, the Sunshine style lettering lacks its usual robust 'old gold' look, so there may have been some colour degradation after the image was taken. The official colour of express passenger locomotive lining and lettering was old gold and it is hard to believe that this ensemble was painted in the same colours as the altogether brighter shades of green and yellow seen in the previous view. No.30740 received BR green livery in May 1950 and was withdrawn in December 1955.* (The late S.C.Townroe - Ref: SR34)

ABOVE: *R.W.Urie introduced several different 4-6-0 designs for the LSWR, all of which were to be of some significance in the future evolution of British steam. The express passenger N15s have been covered but the earliest type to appear were actually the H15 Class of 1914, the first ever British mixed traffic 4-6-0s with outside Walschaerts valve gear and 6ft driving wheels. Some were built new in both LSWR and SR days, while others were rebuilt from Drummond 4-6-0s, again in both LSWR and SR times, including No.332 seen pausing at Winchester with a down local train in Summer 1938. This example is one of the five Southern rebuilds of Drummond Class F13 4-6-0s carried out in 1924/5 at Eastleigh works; they all retained the Drummond pattern 'watercart' tenders with inside bearings and very visible wheels. No.332 was fitted with smoke deflectors in 1930. It carries the standard dark green livery in this view and is hauling a typical three-coach set of LSWR non-corridor coaches with lavatories, plus two vans in the rear.* (Philip Colebourn Collection)

BELOW: *This broadside portrait of LSWR H15 4-6-0 No.483 taken at Eastleigh in April 1938, is probably one of the most accurate colour records in existence of the later pattern of Maunsell green livery as applied to larger passenger engines. The colour itself is not quite perfect but the minutiae of the lining out style is very clearly shown. Both wheels and cylinders are green, with black axle ends on the former and a lined panel on the latter. The footsteps on both engine and tender are also lined green. Only a month after this picture was taken the first Bulleid livery experiments commenced. This engine is one of the original Urie examples which set the standard for his straightforward two-cylinder big engine policy. Eleven examples of this type with shallow driving wheel splashers were built in 1914 (including the one rebuild) and another fifteen were built/rebuilt by the Southern Railway with various Maunsell modifications, including straight running plates. The six H15 rebuilds were of older Drummond 4-6-0s, No.335 by the LSWR and Nos.330-4 by the Southern.* (Colour-Rail - Ref: SR8)

OPPOSITE, ABOVE: *Douglas Earle Marsh produced two similar classes of 4-4-2 (Atlantics) for the LB&SCR based on Ivatt's large boilered design for the GNR. The original batch of five unsuperheated locomotives was built by Kitsons in 1905/6 and classified H1, followed in 1911/12 by six Brighton built superheated class H2s. By 1948, only three of the earlier class survived and one of them had been modified (some would say mutilated) by Bulleid to provide a test bed for the sleeve valve arrangement intended for his Leader Class; so it was the later H2 Class that the colour photographers of the late 1940s managed to record. This first view shows No.2421* South Foreland *at Newhaven shed in 1947, recently repainted in post-war Malachite green with black and yellow lining. As seen here, the cab front seems to be black, a detail aspect of the post-war Bulleid livery which still remains a debated point, some sources maintaining that cab fronts were green with this style. Cylinders, wheels and footsteps are plain black. As BR No.32421 it was condemned in August 1956.* (C.C.B.Herbert - Ref: SR47)

OPPOSITE, BELOW: *This picture was taken at Newhaven shed in June 1949, but there is no evidence of BR ownership on Class H2 No.2425* Trevose Head, *sporting an increasingly grubby coat of Malachite green paint. Once again, the cab front appears to be black, but being in shadow (as often the case), one cannot be certain. As with the final view in the King Arthur section, the lining could be taken for black and white and the shade of green more subdued. During the summer months the surviving Atlantics enjoyed a brief return to glory on the Newhaven relief boat trains, as well as Brighton to London Bridge and Bournemouth services, while Summer Saturdays saw extra work on inter-Regional trains to and from Brighton. The first to go was No.2423 in 1949, but No.2425 lasted until 1956. Both the class and the British 'Atlantic' became extinct when No.32424 was withdrawn in April 1958.* (Colour-Rail - Ref: SR14)

BELOW: *A Maunsell Class U 2-6-0 No.1611 stands at Guildford, around 12.15pm, with the Margate to Birkenhead cross-country service in early autumn 1938. Any passenger wishing to make the whole journey would face a nine hour plus marathon, so it was fortunate that there was a Restaurant Car all the way, serving Breakfast, Luncheon and Tea. An interesting comentary on the times is given by the nature of the (presumably holiday-makers') luggage being loaded. The locomotive is still in Maunsell green with 'Southern' branding and number on the tender. The leading coach, Maunsell Brake Third No.2759 from set No.228, has recently been repainted in Bulleid Malachite green - SR and GWR stock worked the service on alternate week days. Finally, the crew do not seem unduly concerned by the electrified third rail - the white patch on the end of the wooden casing appears to be the only warning.* (The late Sydney Perrier, courtesy C.S.Perrier - Ref: SR53)

OPPOSITE, ABOVE: *The Schools or V Class 4-4-0s were not only Maunsell's success-ful design, they could also lay sound claim to be the finest new design ever introduced by the Southern and they were certainly one of the most outstanding 4-4-0s of all time. Built especially for the restricted gauge Hastings line this three-cylinder class quickly proved itself equal to many of the Southern 4-6-0 types and it is no accident that BR put them into the 5P classification, the only 4-4-0s to be thus distinguished. A total of 40 examples was built between 1930 and 1935 and in this atmospheric view, one of the 1934 examples, No.929* Malvern *passes a magnificent array of LSWR pattern signals as it arrives at Eastleigh station in 1938, hauling the well known Bournemouth-Birkenhead through train composed of GWR stock. As with the Margate-Birkenhead train, Southern and Great Western rakes worked the service on alternate days. No.929 is still in its original Maunsell dark green livery but in June 1938 it was given an early example of Bulleid's new Malachite green.* (Pendragon Collection - Ref: SR63)

OPPOSITE, BELOW: *When first built, the Schools did not carry smoke deflectors and at first glance, this engine appears to be in that condition; but it is merely illusory, the smoke shields being somewhat obscured in the background. However, the angle of view allows some idea to be gained of the original configuration. The engine is the first of the 1932 batch: No.910* Merchant Taylors, *and is leaving Tunbridge Wells Central on a wet day in late 1939 with exactly the sort of service for which it was designed - a down Hastings train. It received the Malachite green livery seen here in August 1939 and carried it until November 1942. Though not quite as sharp as some images in this survey, the early unshaded Bulleid tender lettering can be distinguished and the smoke deflectors are mostly green, in which latter respect, the engine makes an interesting comparison with the contemporary view of King Arthur No.789 at Templecombe, earlier in this chapter. After the war No.910 remained in wartime Southern black until it was repainted BR lined black in December 1948. The leading coach is No.3235, one of a 1932 Maunsell three-coach set No.940, built to the restricted 8ft width especially for the Hasting line.* (The late Sydney Perrier, courtesy C.S.Perrier - Ref: SR55)

BELOW: *No.905* Tonbridge, *illustrated here at Eastleigh in 1948, first appeared in May 1930 as one of the first ten to be built. The Schools were the last 4-4-0s to be built in mainland Britain and almost the last in the British Isles, but there were a few Irish examples still to appear. In this picture, the engine carries its December 1946 coat of Malachite green paint, with what appear to be earlier unshaded tender lettering, though this may be an illusion. What is undoubted is that the engine has green wheels, albeit dirty, and there is not much doubt that the cab front is black - see earlier captions regarding the Marsh Atlantics. It was to be September 1949 before Tonbridge received BR No.30905 and lined black livery. In August 1958 it was repainted in BR green which it carried until withdrawal in December 1961.* (The late S.C.Townroe - Ref SR31)

ABOVE: *Dorchester shed in the first year of Nationalisation and Schools Class No.922* Marlborough *(one of the 1933 batch of ten engines) awaits a return working to its home depot. It is in post war Malachite green livery with half green smoke deflectors, black cylinders and very dirty green wheels. This time, the shaded 'Sunshine' lettering does show and once again, there is little evidence of any green paint on the cab front. An interesting point to make is that by this time, approximately half the Schools had been given Lemaitre multiple exhaust and large diameter chimneys by Bulleid, but none of the four examples depicted here were thus modified.* (The late S.C.Townroe - Ref: SR35)

OPPOSITE, ABOVE: *The three constituents of the SR all possessed a number of 4-4-0 types, though those of LB&SCR origin were not amongst the best. But this could not be said of the LSWR 4-4-0s, which were generally better than that company's 4-6-0s (Urie's designs excepted) and did much valuable work during Southern days. As Stroudley before him had done on the Brighton line, Dugald Drummond brought the 'Scottish School' of locomotive design tradition and style to southern England when he became Locomotive Superintendent of the LSWR in 1895. It is exemplified here by Class L11 4-4-0 No.408, one of a series of 40 locomotives built between 1903 and 1907. The design was effectively a marriage of the successful T9 boiler to a stretched version of the 5ft 7in driving wheel K10 4-4-0 chassis and resulted in a very capable mixed traffic type of very pleasing outline and proportion. In this superb 1936 view, No.408 is newly ex-works at Eastleigh in an immaculately presented Maunsell green livery which the colour film of the time seems to have rendered with extraordinary accuracy. The green wheels with black axle ends can be readily distinguished, as can the black topped front splasher by contrast with the lined out treatment of the combined cab front/trailing splasher top.* (Philip Colebourn Collection)

OPPOSITE, BELOW: *As he had done in Scotland, so too in England, Drummond continued to develop the 4-4-0 type. His early T9 type was probably the most celebrated passenger version, but when train weights began to increase, something bigger was needed which emerged in the shape of twenty Class L12 4-4-0s from Nine Elms Works in 1904/5. The general style was similar to the last batch of T9s (ie with full width combined splashers rather than separate ones for the coupling rods) but the engines had larger boilers, giving an altogether more massive appearance, No.423 appearing in November 1904. The fitting of superheaters and extended smokeboxes from 1915 onwards gave the class a rather ungainly appearance, particularly noticeable in this broadside view. No.423 (superheated in 1919) has the LSWR pattern chimney without capuchon and retains its Drummond pattern double bogie tender. This 1938 shot taken at Eastleigh again shows an engine in spotless Maunsell livery; at its next repaint in October 1940 the Maunsell green was retained but there was no lining out and the new Bulleid style characters were applied with the number transferred to the cabside in place of the former cast plate.* (Philip Colebourn Collection)

OPPOSITE, ABOVE: *In spite of having some Maunsell 2-6-0s, The SE&CR was very much a 4-4-0 line and amongst the more noteworthy types were those designed by Harry Wainwright, and of these, his Class D engines were amongst the most elegant of all time. Here, despite being painted in the rather drab Maunsell dark green, the graceful lines of the D Class are beautifully displayed by No.1092 at Ashford shed in September 1937. The livery does have some interesting variations: the top of the tender is painted unlined green, including the later coal guards fitted to the flared top, the tender frames are lined green. Unfortunately in this view the wheels and wheel centre colours are unclear. The brass splasher beading has been painted over; originally the ornate SE&CR livery also included a polished brass dome.* (The late J.P.Mullett - Ref: SR25)

The long exposure time necessary with early colour film gives an almost painted quality to this image of D Class 4-4-0 No.1726 standing against the background blur of carriages and steam. It was taken in the Chatham side at Victoria c.1937 and the locomotive may well be working back towards Ashford, its home depot, via Maidstone East. There are a number of differences in the livery when compared with the previous view, the beading on the rear splasher is lined black and white as are the coupling rod splashers, and the tender is painted in the more usual 'Eastleigh' style with large black border and plain black frames. The front splasher tops on both engines are black, but it is unclear where this gives way to the green colour of the cab front, maybe just below the handrail. No.1726 was the first member of the unrebuilt Ds to be condemned, in November 1947, but sister engine, No.1737 is preserved as SE&CR No.737 at the National Railway Museum. (Philip Colebourn Collection)

BELOW: *Maunsell himself was of SE&CR origin but he was also something of a diplomat, which may be a reason why the Southern steam locomotive livery was based on that of the LSWR. He was also, as has been mentioned in connection with the LSWR 4-6-0s, more than willing to develop good designs from all the Southern constituents. Thus it was that between 1921 and 1927, Maunsell rebuilt 21 of Wainwright's D Class 4-4-0s with superheated Belpaire boilers and modern valves and cylinders. Classified D1 they proved highly successful and together with the similar E1 rebuilds, helped to improve Chatham line services. Dover based D1 No.1727, rebuilt in 1922, is seen here in ex-works condition at Ashford c.1937.*

These rebuilds, along with the similar looking L1 Class 4-4-0s built new by the Southern (and quite a number of other Southern types for that matter), shared strong 'Derby' (Midland Railway) visual lines, largely because Maunsell's chief draughtsman, James Clayton, was of Midland origin. But there is little doubt that the Maunsell inside cylinder 4-4-0s (rebuilt or new) were better machines than the feeble LMS Class 2Ps which they much resembled. Note the plain coupling rods, a distinguishing feature between this class and the L1s and E1s. The Maunsell green is particularly dark in this dull weather shot making the wheels appear black; they are in fact green. (Philip Colebourn Collection)

These two pictures show ex-South Eastern Railway (one half of the SE&CR system) Stirling Class F1 4-4-0 No.1043 before and during a visit to Ashford works. The first view was taken at Reading Southern shed in August 1937 and finds No.1043 in rather dirty external condition which cannot hide the Victorian origins of the design, particularly the tender, though the engine is shown in Wainwright's rebuilt form of 1903, rather than the original 1883 configuration. There is some evidence of lining out around the cut outs in the tender frames although it is impossible to establish the base colour. James Stirling, brother of the more famous Patrick of the GNR, came to the SER from the Glasgow and South Western and there was more than a hint of G&SWR styling in his SER designs - a further example of the Scottish influence on the Southern constituents to add to that of Stroudley and Drummond. Stirling's own style is especially well seen on the locomotive behind No.1043, Class R 0-6-0T No.1070 of 1888,

retaining domeless boiler and smokebox wing plates; its livery is probably unlined black.

In the second picture, taken only one month later at Ashford Works, we see No.1043 resplendent in newly acquired dark green livery. Both the wheel and coupling rod splasher tops are black, the latter being plain green on the outer faces as before. The tops of the frames above the running plate are also green, the splasher beading is painted over and on the cab area the beading remains unlined. The black/green divide comes at the angle between cab front and rear splasher top while the wheels are all-over green without black centres. A 'Not to be moved target' on the smokebox suggests that work is not yet complete; the boiler handrail and coupling rods will presumably be polished. In the background the 3500 gallon tender of Class U 2-6-0 No.1626 gives a good illustration of both the lining and lettering of the modern style flat sided tenders. (Colour-Rail and the late J.P.Mullett - Refs: SR12; SR28)

The London, Brighton & South Coast was largely a short haul passenger railway operating in an area neatly described by its name. Along with all the other railways operating in SE England, freight traffic was never as important to the balance sheet as it was in other areas of the country. Consequently the largest freight locomotives the LB&SC operated were seventeen Class K 2-6-0s to a 1913 design by L.B.Billinton. With 5ft 6in wheels they were well suited to excursion traffic as well, giving a useful extra motive power option in the summer months - and indeed, when they all came to BR they were classified as a mixed traffic type. This good looking design is represented in this photograph by No.2346 posing outside Eastleigh shed in April 1938. The livery is Maunsell dark green with black and white lining; in this case the cylinders are lined green, whilst the wheels appear black, as does the Westinghouse pump. Note how quickly the lining has deteriorated on the firebox bands. (Colour-Rail - Ref: SR10)

This fine line up of four Southern locomotives was taken at Ashford in Summer 1939. The leading engine, U Class 2-6-0 No.1613, is coupled to a 4000 gallon tender with sloping tops to the side sheets, received a year or so earlier. Next in line is SE&CR Class J 0-6-4T No.1598, one of a small class of five engines designed by Wainwright for passenger work (below). Behind, is another Wainwright type, H Class 0-4-4T No.1305, while bringing up the rear is Class N 2-6-0 No.1825. Built in 1923, it completed some 40 years service before withdrawal in October 1963. It has a 3500 gallon tender and like all the Maunsell 2-6-0s was fitted with smoke deflectors in the mid-1930s. In spite of apparent appearances, all the locomotives are painted green. (Pendragon Collection - Ref: SR61)

The Class C 0-6-0 goods engine, dating from 1900, was one of the first designs to appear after the formation of the SE&CR and under Wainwright's supervision, though it bore more than a hint of Stirling in terms of styling, he having been succeeded by Wainwright on the SER only a year or so earlier in 1899 and just before the SE&CR working arrangement was drawn up. As the standard SE&CR goods type, well over 100 were built - a considerable number of repeats of the same design for this part of the railway system. In this view, No.1268, dating from 1904, is ex-works from Ashford and seen outside Ashford shed in September 1937. The livery is plain black, modestly relieved by the bold Southern markings and the red backed numberplate on the cabside. (The late J.P.Mullett - Ref: SR24)

Robert Urie built five of these powerful and impressive Class H16 4-6-2 tanks for the LSWR in 1921/2. Despite being mainly employed on London area freight services, they were painted green, presumably because they sometimes worked ECS duties out of Waterloo. BR on the other hand afforded nothing more than plain black, except No.30520 which was lined out in the early days of Nationalisation. No.516 is seen here at Eastleigh in April 1938 *carrying Maunsell green livery, with smaller 15in numerals applied. By the late 1930s, elaborately lined out liveries were the exception rather than the rule, and for locomotives generally working on goods duties something of a rarity. The smokebox on the left hand side is that of Class H15 4-6-0 No.483, seen earlier in this chapter and photographed on the same day.* (Philip Colebourn Collection)

Following the success of his final 4-4-2 tank design, the I3 class, D.E.Marsh designed two even larger express passenger 4-6-2 tanks for the LB&SCR which came out in 1910 and 1912. The 1910 version, No.325 Abergavenny, was classified J1 and had inside Stephenson valve gear. The second machine Class J2 No.326 Bessborough appeared after Marsh's retirement and was given outside Walschaerts valve gear. Lawson Billinton, successor to Marsh, chose to enlarge still further on the theme and eventually produced seven Class L 4-6-4 tanks, later rebuilt to Class N15X 4-6-0s following the electrification of the SR Central Section main line in the mid 1930s. Fortunately both of the Marsh 4-6-2 tank engines were photographed in colour, by now displaying the rounded roof form which the Southern gave them in 1928 in succession to the original more rectilinear shape; the Southern had also painted out the original names when the engines first lost their old LB&SCR umber livery.

For a pair of 'one-offs', these two engines enjoyed a remarkable c.40 year lifespan, both being withdrawn in 1951. In the first view, Class J1 No.2325 displays its massive but elegant proportions at Eastleigh in April 1938. It is painted in Maunsell dark green with 'Southern' branding and the number placed centrally on the tank side; note the lined green panel on the cylinders and more unusually the lined green Westinghouse pump. The equally handsome J2 No.2326 was seen in September 1947 at Tunbridge Wells West shed, home depot to both engines during this period. It sports post-war Malachite livery with Sunshine lettering and the number now transferred to the bunker side, which it retained when first given BR No.32326 and it may even have been scrapped in that style. Once again - see some earlier views - the Malachite livery and its bright yellow lining and insignia appear rather restrained in colour compared with other views in this chapter, so some deterioration of the film emulsion may have occurred. (J.M.Jarvis - Refs: SR9; SR18)

ABOVE: *Another inherited large passenger tank design was the SE&CR Class J 0-6-4 type, seen here in the shape of No.1597 heading a down train near Bromley South in June 1937. It was one of a small class of five engines designed by Wainwright in 1913 for heavier duty work and which survived into BR days, although by the end of 1951 all had been withdrawn. Like the Brighton 4-6-2Ts (above) they succumbed to the arrival of new 2-6-4Ts of both LMS and BR standard design. The locomotive is working bunker first with only a modest load in tow: a SE&CR three-coach 'birdcage' set, so named because of the raised roof lookouts at the brake ends and typical of the pre-group non-corridor stock which continued to be used on many SR steam services (railway or region) until electrification. The locomotive livery is Maunsell dark green and gives sight of the painted rear end numerals, applied to the bunker not the buffer plank; note too that the flared top to the bunker is unlined green. Taken from the bottom of his garden, this picture is a very rare colour image by that well known and much travelled photographer Henry Casserley.* (The late H.C.Casserley - Ref: SR42)

OPPOSITE, ABOVE: *Drummond's versatile Class M7 0-4-4 tanks, dating from 1897 and built over a period until 1911, are represented here by No.51 standing at Bournemouth shed in 1939. It is resplendent in immaculate dark green livery and the number in applied in 15in numerals rather than the standard 18in pattern; the lettering is the normal 6½in type. The picture gives a very good rendition of both the green itself and the typical Southern 'old gold' insignia of the time. Unlike some tank classes, the front of the side tanks are lined green, not black, though the post-war Malachite livery specified these areas to be black. Built in 1905, No.51 was fitted with push-pull equipment in 1930 - note the air reservoir under the front bufferbeam and the extra vacuum pipes. Well over 100 of these engines were built (again a large class by Southern pre- or post-group standards) and they enjoyed a long life, all but one reaching BR and most lasting until the 1960s. As BR No.30051, this engine was not condemned until September 1962 and was almost 60 years old at the time.* (The late S.C.Townroe - Ref: SR29)

OPPOSITE, BELOW: *Another long-lived 0-4-4T on the Southern was the Wainwright Class H of which 66 examples were constructed at Ashford between 1904 and 1915, with No.1265 appearing in 1905, one of ten built in that year with straight sided bunkers. This picture was taken at Stewarts Lane in 1939, the engine being engaged in shunting coal wagons. The livery is once again Maunsell dark green, the numerals being almost too big for the tank sides of this small design. Also worthy of note is the black paint on the front of the tanks and on top of the splashers. The wheels seem also to be finished in black, though as often the case, this detail cannot really be confirmed either way. All but two of the class reached BR and along with many others, No.1265 was fitted with push-pull equipment in the BR period, a process which started in 1949 though it was 1958 before this engine was modified (now BR No.31265); it was not to run long in this new form, being scrapped in 1960.* (Philip Colebourn Collection)

This attractive view at Ashford shed c.1937 is dominated by the stylish outline of Class R1 0-4-4T No.1703, built in 1900 as a slightly enlarged version (bigger bunker capacity and larger bogie wheels) of Kirtley's 1891 Class R design for the London Chatham and Dover Railway (the other half of the SE&CR). It is seen in company with Class N 2-6-0 No.1865 of the 1925 SR-built batch, using parts made by Woolwich Arsenal, and an unidentified Class C 0-6-0; note the reporting number discs on all three engines. The 0-4-4T has degraded olive green Maunsell livery and by now is carrying a Wainwright Class H type boiler, the interchange capability being no doubt one reason why all but two lasted until early BR days. No.1703 was the penultimate survivor, lasting until 1954 as BR No.31703 and by that time fitted with push-pull gear. (Philip Colebourn Collection)

Although, like the LSWR, the LB&SCR had some 0-4-4Ts of distinctly 'Scottish' outline, built by Marsh, the far more typical four-coupled passenger tank on the Brighton system during much of its life was Stroudley's Class D1 0-4-2T design of 1873, of which this veteran, No.2299, was not only one of the oldest examples but also one of a small handful to reach BR (just!). It started life as No.6 Wimbledon in 1874, being renumbered 76 in 1907 and 299 in 1909. Of typically Stroudley outline, some 112 of the original 125 built reached the Southern, many being already 50 years old at the time, and withdrawal was steady thereafter. A number were push-pull fitted and sub-classified D1/M. No.2299 was one such and is seen here out of use at Eastleigh in 1948. Its degraded Maunsell livery was at least ten years old and the engine was scrapped only a year later, possibly never having been steamed again after this picture was taken. This picture is undoubtedly one of very few colour images to show a retained pre-war livery in early BR days. (The late S.C.Townroe - Ref: SR26)

It is perhaps appropriate that the last specifically passenger class to feature in the Southern part of this survey should be 'Brighton Terrier' 0-6-0Ts, for these engines were surely amongst the most popular of all Southern engines of any type. The Terriers, more formally Class A, later A1 (A1X if fitted with Marsh boilers after 1911), were introduced by Stroudley in 1872 as lightweight passenger engines for the many London suburban routes of the LB&SCR with less than perfect track. For many years they were also particularly associated with the Hayling Island branch, their light axle loading allowing them to cross the rather delicate wooden structure of the Langstone Viaduct which connected the island with the mainland.

The bay platform at Havant is the location for the first view which shows No.2644 on a Hayling Island service in August 1937. No.2644 was built in June 1877 as LB&SCR No.44 Fulham and rebuilt as A1X in 1912, by which date it was already on the duplicate list as

No.644. It was renumbered B644 by the Southern Railway and after 1931 this was altered to 2644, both the B (for Brighton) and the addition of 2000 to the number indicating an ex-LB&SCR locomotive. In July 1948 it received BR No.32644 and plain black livery inscribed 'British Railways' in full and it was eventually withdrawn in April 1951.

The second view captures a rather dirty Class A1X No.2661 on the island at Hayling North in April 1938. Once again the livery is Maunsell green. Built as No.61 Sutton by the LB&SCR in 1875, it became A1X in 1912 and continued working for both the Southern and BR until April 1963; later that same year the Hayling Island branch closed. From May 1951 No.32661 carried BR lined black livery and is now preserved on the Kent and East Sussex Railway. (The late Sydney Perrier, courtesy C.S.Perrier and G.J.Jefferson - Refs: SR45; SR23)

Confusingly, the R/R1 classification was not only used by the SE&CR for the former LC&DR 0-4-4Ts (above) but also for two 0-6-0 tank engine variants of SER origin and neither the SE&CR nor the SR sorted things out later - perhaps everyone knew the difference who needed to, for the Southern always displayed a somewhat cavalier approach to the many duplicated letter classifications of its inherited fleet - and added a few more of its own for good measure! Be that as it may, the Stirling Class R 0-6-0Ts dated from 1888 and No.1155 was one of those built ten years later. It is seen pausing during shunting operations at Ashford in 1939, and was one of six to have been given a cut down chimney and altered whistle position in order to bring them within the restricted loading gauge of the historic Canterbury & Whitstable line; but it still retains the original Stirling style of domeless boiler. The livery is plain black with Maunsell characters. By this date only four members of the class were still at work and No.1155 was withdrawn later the same year; the last survivor No.1124 succumbed in 1943. (Philip Colebourn Collection)

The Class R1 0-6-0Ts were SE&CR rebuilds of the original R Class, thirteen of the original 25 being so converted between 1910 and 1922 with domed boilers and 'Pagoda' cab, some later reverting to rounded cab and being given shorter chimneys, again for the Whitstable branch. In this unusual view, a plain black R1 No.1154 (rebuilt 1912) shunts at Folkestone Harbour in 1938; prominent is a typical wood-planked four-wheel Southern passenger luggage van, essentially to the SE&CR design and destined to be built with little change until well into BR days. The R1s themselves became famous for their pyrotechnic exploits working trains up the fearsome gradient of the Folkestone Harbour branch, two, or more often three and four at a time. The thirteen locomotives surviving in 1938 all passed into BR ownership and their association with the line did not end until May 1959 when GWR Pannier tanks completely took over the Harbour branch. The last survivor No.31047 was withdrawn from Nine Elms shed in March 1960. (The late Sydney Perrier, courtesy C.S.Perrier - Ref: SR52)

The LB&SCR Class E1 0-6-0T was introduced in 1874 for goods working. Larger than the perhaps more famous 'Terriers', they displayed very similar lines and they were the goods equivalent of the Class D 0-4-2Ts already considered. In this picture, goods status notwithstanding, old No.152, originally named Hungary *and dating from 1880, is seen in somewhat degraded Maunsell lined green livery at Newport IOW in the late 1930s. It was one of four members of the class sent to the Isle of Wight by the Southern Railway, mainly to assist with goods services. After transfer to the island in July 1932 it was numbered W2 and received the name* Yarmouth, *this time by way of an attractive cast nameplate rather than the older painted style (which had vanished long before Southern days). No.W2 was the first of the island's E1s to be withdrawn in 1956.* (Pendragon Collection)

The E1s were built over a long period between 1874 and 1891 to the tune of 79 examples - and this was one of the last batch of five, built in 1891 as No.160 Portslade. *Seen here with Marsh pattern boiler at Eastleigh in 1948, No.2160 is carrying the standard post-war Bulleid goods livery and this is the only even half reasonable colour view which has been found of that style - and even then it is none too clear. The engines were plain black, while the insignia were, like those on the contemporary passenger livery, of the so-called sunshine style; but in the case of black engines, the back shading had Malachite green highlights rather than the bright yellow of the passenger types, though this is hardly obvious! On this engine, insignia are of the smaller type. The engine itself was withdrawn in 1951 though it was ten more years before the class became extinct, save for one fortuitously preserved example, old No.110* Burgundy, *sold out of service by the Southern as early as 1927.* (The late S.C.Townroe - Ref: SR27)

The Southern section of this survey is concluded by this picture taken in 1939 near Norwood Junction, for it offers an excellent summation of many of those characteristics which made the SR distinctively different. In it can be seen steam, diesel and electric power, all intermixed. The steam scene, unusually for the Southern, is represented by a goods train, though the motive power is quite typical of the company - a pre-group engine, which in this case takes the form of ex-LB&SCR Billinton Class E3 0-6-2T No.2167, dating from 1894. In the right middle distance can be seen a suburban multiple unit electric train consisting, as did most pre-war Southern suburban emus, of re-worked pre-group locomotive hauled stock, in this case SE&CR.

To the left can be seen 350HP 0-6-0 diesel-electric shunting locomotive No.2, one of three built at Ashford in 1937 using English Electric equipment. It later became BR No.15202 and it is often forgotten that the now familiar diesel shunter had its origins during the pre-war company period. Although the LMS was the largest user of this new type of traction in company days, examples of the type (which eventually evolved into the ubiquitous BR Class 08 engines) were obtained by all members of the Big Four. (The late Sydney Perrier, courtesy C.S.Perrier - Ref: SR56)

CHAPTER SIX

THE YEARS OF CHANGE 1948-50

Though not literally within the time frame of this chapter, this view taken at North Woolwich in April 1951 is absolutely typical of the random mixture of livery styles which were seen during the years of transition - note, for example, the mixture of teak fished and red and cream coaches. The locomotive, in charge of an RCTS special, is former Great Eastern Railway (LNER Class J69) 0-6-0T No. E8619. The engine is in post war LNER apple green livery with Gill Sans insignia and although it is now over three years since nationalisation, the engine still carries the temporary 'E' prefix to its LNER number, a reminder of the interim measure adopted only during the first few months of 1948 until the complete BR renumbering system was evolved. It later became BR No.68619, but remained green until 1953. This was because it had been selected as the Liverpool Street station pilot in January 1948, the date of painting into the style seen here, and was always well looked after in consequence. Its subsequent BR liveries were also interesting. After a short period in plain BR black (the 'standard' livery for the type), it was then given the fully lined BR black livery with red side rods and polished metalwork, along with Class N7 0-6-2T No.69614 which performed similar duties at Liverpool Street. Finally, in 1959, it was repainted GER blue with red lining and side rods. (T.B.Owen - Ref: BRE412)

Introduction

Quite naturally, one of the most interesting aspects of the nationalisation of the railways in 1948, at least as far as bystanders were concerned, was the matter of the new liveries to be carried. Speculation was intense and even at the very highest level of the British Transport Commission (BTC), the subject was clearly given considerable attention. The new BR locomotive chief, Robert A.Riddles, one time personal assistant to William Stanier of the LMS, certainly had a view himself and he it was who recounted some of the background detail to the editor of this book in reply to a question why the old LMS liveries had not (apparently) been thought worthy of consideration by the new organisation. The story has been recounted elsewhere but is still worth the re-telling.

It was Riddles' view (he was no mean psychologist!) that, given the mainly LMS origins of the top BR locomotive management, it would be unwise to suggest any form of LMS locomotive livery for the whole system. As he put it: "We were getting most of our own way everywhere else!" He was also surely mindful of the LMS experience in 1923 when Midland methods and colour schemes were instituted in the new company without any form of debate and with unsatisfactory results.

In the event, blue and green were the only hues considered for the more important engines, it being presumed that goods engines would remain black. To this end, a few locomotives from all four regions were painted in various blue or green shades, together with different styles of lining, and then re-entered service to 'gauge public reaction'. Much the same applied to carriages and a number of 'sets' of coaches received experimental liveries. But most interesting were the so-called 'beauty parades' which were organised at an early stage and at which were displayed examples of the various schemes under consideration for the benefit of the new BTC Chairman Sir Cyril, later Lord Hurcomb.

The most celebrated of the parades was undoubtedly that which took place at Addison Road Station, Kensington on 30th January 1948 and which involved, amongst other items, a number of LMS Class 5 4-6-0s, decked out in three shades of green (LNER, GWR and SR, each with appropriate lining). On the completion of the run-past, Hurcomb asked Riddles if he (Riddles) had anything else to show him. Now Riddles had a fine sense of humour and, unbeknown to his chairman, had (so he told the writer) instructed Crewe Works to do a 'real paint job' on yet another Class 5 which he duly summoned up from "round the corner" as he put it. When it appeared it was seen to be in a magnificent rendition of the London and North Western Railway 'blackberry black' livery, with all brightwork polished and gleaming. "Riddles, you b.....d!" is reputed to have been the chairman's comment, Riddles, of course, being an ex-LNWR man himself. "As a result of which," said Riddles to the writer, "I managed to get more than 19,000 out of 20,000 engines painted black - which is what I had wanted all along!"

Of course, not all the black engines were given lining but the LNWR style was adopted as the BR 'intermediate' livery and many classes were eventually to carry it - usually to very good effect. Naturally, the principal express types were given 'coloured' liveries and at first two schemes were in evidence - blue with black and white lining (somewhat akin to the old Caledonian livery) for the very largest types and GWR middle chrome green (with GWR style lining) for the other express classes, though the latter shade was renamed BR standard green to avoid any lingering regional sensitivities! It was not an unqualified aesthetic success on many of the designs to which it was applied.

The combination of the new standard liveries, together with many different examples of transitional styles, made the first few years after 1947 especially interesting to the lineside observer and fortunately, many of the variations were recorded in colour. In the following pages we have put most views in the same company order as in previous chapters but again it must be stated that the balance is somewhat uneven, former LNER and SR classes being better covered than LMS and GWR types. In part this is because the GWR types mostly remained unchanged but also because colour photography was still relatively new and many colour photographers understandably concentrated on the 'non-black' types. This means that many interesting post-1947 experimental liveries in the former LMS fleet were never recorded in colour, including several 4-6-2s and three-cylinder 4-6-0s which also ran in 'LNWR' colours for a while. Nevertheless, we have been able to embrace all the significant styles, if not necessarily for all regions.

Except on former GWR locomotives, which retained their cast numberplates, the new BR standard numerals (essentially the final LNER Gill Sans style) were given to all types, along with LMS pattern front numberplates with Gill Sans figures. The blue livery was abandoned in 1951 (it was said not to have lasting quality) and GWR green became the only non-black livery thereafter, save for a few red ex-LMS pacifics from 1957 onwards. Although these later changes are outside the theme of this book, we have thought fit to include some examples of the BR 'standard' blue style since it was in practice of a temporary nature. We have also, for the same reason, included views of engines in BR standard livery lettered BRITISH RAILWAYS in full; this form of identity was only used until the adoption of the Lion and Wheel tender/tank-side emblem in 1949.

Robert Riddles' 'show-stopper', Class 5 4-6-0 No.45292 stands in Marylebone station on 6th April 1948 sporting a livery which was to become very familiar over the next 20 years or so: black with LNWR style red, cream and grey lining. In the case of No.45292 this included the LNWR black edge on the bufferbeam, which was not repeated. The firebox is also lined in double red along with the boiler; the standard BR lined black left the firebox area plain. Both cab and tender characters are painted in cream/straw coloured sans serif characters. Note how the lining is extended over the cab windows, not forming the more familiar panel below. Likewise, the tender is lined closer to the panel edges than was later to become normal. The engine first received this livery at Crewe in late January 1948. The visible stock is LMS in plain red (non-corridor stock behind the engine, later to become the standard colour for this type of vehicle) and plum and spilt milk (gangwayed coaches in the background and not adopted as standard); coach numbers are placed at the right hand end of the vehicles. For a time after this all stock was numbered at the left hand end. Other locomotives on display that day were LNER A3 No.60091 and B17 No.61661. Coaching stock also included two GWR coaches in GW livery. (Andrew Dow collection - Ref: BRM1237)

BELOW: *This second view at Marylebone on 6th April 1948 shows one of the short-lived experimental liveries for the second livery demonstration, applied to LNER Class B17/4 4-6-0 No.61661* Sheffield Wednesday. *This was the first locomotive to carry BR experimental light/apple green livery. The lining out was initially yellow, as seen here. Though not shown here, the accompanying A3 pacific on this occasion, No.60091, was painted blue with similar lining. On 26th April 1948 at King's Cross both No.61661 and No.60091 had been relined in red, cream and grey, in similar fashion to Black 5 No.45292. The numbers and lettering on No.61661 are hand painted, the figures on the cabside being rather larger than the later standard. They have the curled top '6' which was a late LNER variation to the true Gill Sans style. The firebox and the rear of the tender are lined out which was not continued by BR, nor was single lining around the windows perpetuated. Although the football below the nameplate is still in place, the club's blue and white colours have been painted out. No.61661, together with No.61665 were used to haul a chocolate and cream liveried set of Gresley stock between Liverpool St and Yarmouth during Summer 1948. In August 1949 both locomotives received BR dark green livery, unusually still with full lettering on the tender rather than the BR symbol.* (Andrew Dow collection - Ref: BRE1006)

OPPOSITE, ABOVE: *Genuine pre-war liveries were somewhat rare by the time of nationalisation but because of generally inadequate maintenance between 1939-45 and the relatively slow improvement thereafter, any engine which had its paintwork in reasonable condition was often left largely alone. Thus it was that a few LMS examples retained their late 1930s crimson lake livery for ten years or more, one such being Jubilee Class 5XP 4-6-0 No 45572* Eire. *In this view it bears LMS red livery with the final pre-war form of insignia (chrome yellow shaded vermilion) on the tender. In spite of the obvious grime, the livery itself has lasted very well and most of the lining is visible. Under the final BR scheme, most ex-LMS engines had 40000 added to their old numbers, Eire being thus treated in August 1948 without full repaint, a common practice at the time. The only obvious change from pure LMS state is the new BR number on both cabside and smokebox door in LMS (1946 style) numerals and the bright vermilion nameplate background - the latter was definitely not LMS practice! The Bristol Barrow Road allocated engine was seen at Chesterfield Midland, hauling a cross country York-Bristol service during winter 1948/9.* (Pendragon Collection - Ref: BRM285)

OPPOSITE, BELOW: *Six LMS Duchesses carried an experimental blue shade, combined with LNWR style red, cream and grey lining, as carried here by No.46241* City of Edinburgh, *photographed at Camden shed in April 1949; the other similarly treated examples were Nos.46224/7/30/1/2/41 and some observers recorded a purple cast to the colour, though this could have been a trick of the light. The engines were repainted in late Spring 1948 to haul the summer experimental liveried trains, in particular the 'Royal Scot' service. On this de-streamlined locomotive there are two bands of cream and grey applied on the front angle of the running plate. The cylinders also have double red lining and the power class 7P is applied below the number on the cab side. Later that summer a further Duchess No.46244* King George VI *was repainted in a lighter shade of blue with yellow and black lining, becoming the first locomotive painted in what became the standard shade, though the lining was altered to white and black in the final standard form. Given that Crewe works was responsible for maintaining the class it is not surprising that LNWR lined black also appeared on some members of the class at this time, although it was never official BR policy to paint express passenger engines in this guise.* (W.H.G.Boot - Ref: BRM139)

ABOVE: *This second shot of a blue Duchess shows the standard livery carried by the majority of the class, if only for a short period in many cases. The massive proportions of these engines is well illustrated in this view of No.46239* City of Chester *departing from Rugby c.1951. It is noticeable how quickly the accumulation of dirt obliterated the lining out, particularly on the boiler, and the generally dull state of the livery does support the view that its lasting quality was not good. Note the early BR symbol on the tender and also that the lettering on the cabside has deteriorated to an 'off-white' shade. The amended power class 8P is now placed above the number, a reminder of the fact that in 1951, some of the LMS passenger power classifications (the whole scheme having been adopted system wide by BR) were changed: 5XP, 6P and 7P becoming the more logical 6P, 7P and 8P respectively.* (NRM Collection)

OPPOSITE, ABOVE: *Rebuilt Patriot Class 6P 4-6-0 (class 7P post-1951 - see previous view) No.5531* Sir Frederick Harrison *stands outside Derby Works about May 1948 having been repainted in experimental apple green. It was converted to taper boilered form in November 1947 and carried 1946 style LMS express passenger livery for a short period. The official instructions for the lining out with this style was the same for those in blue and black - ie LNWR style. But the colour effect seems different, almost chrome orange. Whether this is due to the type of film used or the register of the red applied directly against the rather acid green colour is unknown. Certainly the rendering of the bufferbeams on both visible engines make one believe that vermilion may have been used, this being the LMS colour for such features. The lettering is in straw yellow, the same colour applied to the thin line edging the grey band. Note that handrails, except the rear one on the tender, are painted black. The power classification 6P appears below the cabside number. The cast plates on the smokebox door have been picked out in white paint and the numberplate is a transitional one with bolder figures than subsequently used.* (J.M.Jarvis - Ref: BRM234)

OPPOSITE, BELOW: *Rebuilt Patriot 4-6-0 No.45540* Sir Robert Turnbull *approaches Bletchley with an up express in July 1948. The locomotive was painted experimental green and renumbered at Crewe in May 1948. It was used to work the 8.55am Euston - Wolverhampton and 4.05pm return service, which was made up from LMS stock in experimental plum & spilt milk livery and was one of the services operated in new colours to gauge public reaction - see chapter introduction. No.45540 is seen with the 4.05pm up train in the July evening sunshine and the 'against the light' viewpoint obscures some of the detail. But it also reveals how the same livery (No.45540 was painted identically to No.45531 in the previous view) can appear to be a quite different shade to the camera, depending on the direction of the light. No.45540 is believed to have been based at Bushbury shed (3B) at the time, along with No.45531* (H.N.James - Ref: BRM25)

ABOVE: *New identification marks on basically unchanged pre-BR liveries were a common feature of the 1948-50 scene and this rear threequarter shot of Class A3 4-6-2 No.60098* Spion Kop *shows one such example, the Doncaster style LNER lining on the back of its tender being especially well seen. The locomotive was one of only a handful of the class which ran with every style of tender which could have been coupled to the A3s. The example shown is the 'New Type' high sided non-corridor tender, No.5481, received in 1943 and kept until withdrawal in October 1963. No.60098 was built as an A3 pacific in 1929 and its original LNER number was 2752. The engine will have backed down into King's Cross station from Top Shed, its home depot, through Gasworks Tunnel. The date is 1949.* (G.J.Jefferson - Ref: BRE334).

OPPOSITE, ABOVE: *This rare view shows the last surviving Hughes L&Y design 4-6-0 (LMS Class 5P) No.50455 standing in York station on the occasion of its final run in revenue service - excursion No.C820 from Blackpool during July 1951. The engine was built under LMS auspices at Horwich in June 1924, having originally been ordered by the L&Y as a 4-6-4T. It was the only member of its class to carry a BR number and was officially withdrawn in October 1951. The shed plate reads 28A, the code for the ex-L&Y Blackpool Central mpd between June 1950 and April 1952. The BR lined black livery is carried in standard form but before the adoption of the tender emblem - a not inappropriate colour scheme for an engine designed by a company whose own livery was rather similar.* (E.Oldham - Ref: BRM 419)

OPPOSITE, BELOW: *A4 Pacific No.60007* Sir Nigel Gresley *stands outside the Rugby Testing Station for the opening ceremonies in October 1948. This plant (a joint LMS/LNER venture initiated before the war) opened officially on 19th October with both this engine and LMS equivalent No.46256* Sir William A.Stanier, FRS *in attendance and No.60007 was the first locomotive to work on the rollers, although not for testing purposes. It is carrying LNER garter blue livery with dark red wheels. The valancing over the coupled wheels and motion was removed during the war to ease maintenance. Both the classification and shed allocation are displayed on the 'bufferbeam'. It has also acquired a BR style front numberplate, with BR Gill Sans number and lettering in the tender in pale cream. Note the curled top to the figure 6 which is not strictly Gill Sans in pattern. Many post war green LNER locomotives carried this style of 6 and 9, and early BR numberplates often perpetuated this error. No.46256 was not photographed on this occasion, possibly because it was still black - see chapter introduction.* (J.M.Jarvis - Ref: BRE158)

OPPOSITE, ABOVE: *A4 4-6-2 No.60028* Walter K.Whigham *was one of four members of the class to be given the experimental blue livery with red, cream and grey lining. The others were Nos.60024/7/9 and all received the livery in June or July 1948. The cabside and tender give the best indication (amongst this collection of images) of the purple tinge which many contemporary observers noted in this colour. The silver-white painted numbers and lettering are applied in Gill Sans style, as is the cast front numberplate. No.60028's home depot King's Cross is still displayed in LNER fashion near the buffers, whilst the classification is now placed under the cabside number. Nos.60028/9 were based at King's Cross shed in Summer 1948 and helped to work the 1.00 pm King's Cross-Edinburgh, coming off at Peterborough; although No.60029 was more often seen on the 'Flying Scotsman'. The other two experimental blue A4s were based at Haymarket and looked after the up 1.45pm service from Edinburgh, as far as Newcastle. Gateshead based blue A3s worked the middle sections. The services were run with coaches in both experimental colour schemes from 21st June, once again as part of the 'public relations' exercise mentioned earlier. No.60028 is captured here at Grantham shed having been turned ready to take an up train in June 1948.* (J.M.Jarvis - Ref: BRE159)

OPPOSITE, BELOW: *This fascinating view at Newcastle Central in 1949, shows A3 No.60084* Trigo *in experimental dark blue livery, initially described by the Railway Observer as Royal Blue, whilst the SLS Journal speaks of a colour approaching Oxford Blue. Many people felt there was a distinct purple tinge in the colour but the colour film of the period was not up to recording such subtleties. One wonders if today's film would fare any better given the vagaries of human perception and lighting. The lining out was LNWR style red, cream and grey with double red lining on the boiler bands. The first experimental blue A3 No.60091 was lined out in yellow and took part in the viewing at Marylebone on 6th April 1948. The lining was altered to the LNWR type and five other A3s were so treated at the end of May 1948: Nos.60045/71/4/5/84. No.60036 was given a lighter shade of blue with similar lining in July. The lettering was in a rich cream colour, rather more yellow than subsequently adopted, which may have misled some of the contemporary observers who also noted the lining as red/yellow. Experimentally liveried A3s were used with specially painted stock on the 1.00pm King's Cross-Edinburgh and 1.45pm Edinburgh-King's Cross services, once again to gauge public reaction to the colours. The coaches were painted in two liveries, plum and off white and chocolate and cream; the full brake behind No.60084 is in the former style. In early June 1949, No.60084 came out from general repair at Doncaster in BR standard blue, which it carried until this was replaced by BR green in August 1952.* (H.N.James - Ref: BRE6)

BELOW: *Despite being the standard livery for only a short period of time, BR blue with black and white lining was applied to all but two of Gresley's non-streamlined pacifics. This shot captures newly repainted A3 No.60072* Sunstar *at York North shed in September 1949. It carried BR blue livery between August 1949 and June 1952. At Nationalisation, No.72 along with No.82 had been the only A3s still in wartime black. All the lined BR liveries omitted lining from the firebox, a departure from LNER practice. However the locomotive's allocation, Heaton, is still displayed in LNER fashion on the bufferbeam. The coaches behind are also interesting: the nearest vehicle is an ex-GCR example in the drab wartime dark brown paint and behind are two Gresley types, one still in varnished teak, the other being a tourist stock brake which has lost its colourful pre-war green and cream livery.* (E.Sanderson - Ref: BRE1120)

ABOVE: *Class A1 Peppercorn Pacific No.60127 provides a stirring sight as it leaves York with a mid day departure for the south in 1949, when the engine was only a few weeks old. These A1s were the last and arguably the best of the LNER pacific designs, undeniably so in maintenance and reliability terms. All were built under BR auspices at Doncaster and Darlington. No.60127 appeared from Doncaster Works during May 1949 in the newly introduced standard blue livery, the first A1 to receive the colour. Prior to No.60127, all the A1s had been given LNER green. The engine was later named* Wilson Worsdell *after the well known NER Locomotive Super-Intendent. North Eastern atmosphere abounds in the generous provision of signalling and the two old sheds in view. On the left is the round-house of York (South) shed and to the right York Queen Street. As yet, there is no sign of new BR carriage colours.* (E.Sanderson - Ref: BRE1115)

OPPOSITE: *These excellent views, taken at Holgate, York in Summer 1949, show LNER Class V2 2-6-2s heading up expresses. From the direction of the light both pictures were taken around 11.00am. In the first No.60835* The Green Howard, Alexandra, The Princess of Wales's Own Yorkshire Regiment *is in charge of an up 'special' working, No.477; note the nameplate backed with the Regimental colours. The locomotive was renumbered into the BR series in April 1948 and was painted in BR lined black during a general repair at Doncaster in July 1948. It has also acquired a smokebox door numberplate, although its allocation, Heaton, is still displayed LNER fashion on the bufferbeam. The tender attached to No.60835 is an older Group Standard type with stepped out coping plates acquired from a D49 in order to save the cost of building a new tender. The stock is all still in LNER livery, led by a flat-sided bogie brake van with horizontal deal boarding. Note too the recently overhauled coach with the white roof, fourth in the rake.*

The second view shows another Heaton engine No.60910 heading south. It received a general repair at Doncaster only a month after No.60835 and so was given the same early BR livery, with fully lettered tender. No.60910 is attached to a more modern flat sided Group Standard tender built at the same time as the locomotive in May 1940. The train is also interesting as it contains an articulated pair of coaches from one of the LNER's streamlined trains still in the original two-tone blue livery. It is probably one of the twins built for the 'Coronation', either a third/brake third pairing or a third/kitchen third which would provide the catering facilities. (E.Sanderson(2) - Refs: BRE1134/1136)

OPPOSITE, ABOVE: *One of the oddly proportioned Thompson 'standard' 6ft 2in A2 pacifics, by now classified A2/3, is caught on camera at Clifton, north of York Station, in 1949. No.60517* Ocean Swell *was built at Doncaster in November 1946 and turned out in lined apple green livery. The locomotive was renumbered into the BR series in August 1948 when it also had 'BRITISH RAILWAYS' in full applied to the tender in sans serif characters but without repaint. It was painted BR green with orange and black lining in February 1950, the A2s being the only 4-6-2s of LNER origin not to receive blue as their first 'official' BR livery; because of their 6ft 2in wheels, they were not, apparently, regarded as a principal express class, though a rather different interpretation of the rules was applied on the Southern 6ft 2in pacifics - see later. The beaded double chimney on No.60517 was later replaced by a lipped variety.* (E.Sanderson - Ref: BRE1115).

OPPOSITE, BELOW: *Gateshead based Peppercorn Class A2 pacific No.E531* Bahram *reverses out of Clifton Carriage Sidings York in Summer 1948. The newly built engine left Doncaster Works in March 1948 in LNER livery, but with BR lettering on the tender and the interim prefix E to its LNER number. It became BR No.60531 in November 1948 and was repainted BR dark green in June 1949, just a few weeks before its transfer to Scotland. No.60531 spent the rest of its career working out of Aberdeen shed and was withdrawn in December 1962. In the background can be seen a pair of LMS Stanier corridor coaches, the one on the right being of post-war build with extra corridor side doors. The rich crimson lake livery has now given way to the more drab post-war maroon shade - or is it simply a case of grime and dirt?* (E.Sanderson - Ref: BRE1116)

BELOW: *Thompson Class B1 4-6-0 No.E1299 enters Aylesbury station with the up 'South Yorkshireman' in August 1948. Both locomotive and train are new. No.E1299 was one of 16 engines turned out by NBL during February and March 1948 with this particular transitional livery, ie. apple green with the E prefix to the number and 'BRITISH RAILWAYS' in full on the tender. No.1287 was the last NBL example to appear with LNER on the tender and No.61304 the first to display its full BR number. The 'South Yorkshireman' was introduced on Monday 31st May 1948 and ran Between Marylebone and Bradford. The down train left London at 4.50pm, the up service at 10.00am. Engines were changed twice en route at Sheffield and Leicester while a locomotive from the LMR worked the Bradford-Sheffield leg.*

No.E1299 went new to Leicester shed in March 1948. The 'Railway Observer' stated that the headboard was cast brass and coach roof boards blue, but this cannot be confirmed by this view. The first four coaches in the rake are of the post-war Thompson type and finished in painted 'teak' LNER style livery but without lining. Later examples were turned out new from 1948 in the first standard BR crimson and cream coach livery. (H.N.James - Ref: BRE9)

Under the LNER 1946 renumbering scheme the GER 4-6-0s returned by coincidence to their original Great Eastern '1500' number series. Thus No.8508 reverted to No.1508. Now carrying BR No.61508 the locomotive is seen at Kittybrewster in September 1949. It was transferred to Scotland in July 1940 and three years later rebuilt to Class B12/4 (see Chapter 2). In all, 25 B12s were transferred to Scotland, although by the date of this picture, several had been withdrawn. Inverurie was keen to implement the LNER's post war directive to paint all its engines green and twenty Scottish B12s received apple green; another unrebuilt example can be spotted in the background. No.61508 received its BR number in October 1948 and was probably repainted from plain black at the same time. Smaller numerals have been painted on the cabside in pale cream. Note too that the coal guard on the tender top is lined green, whilst the Westinghouse pump is black. (J.M.Jarvis - Ref: SC102)

A further Scottish based B12, this time Belpaire boilered No.61502, stands on Keith shed in October 1950 wearing an identical interim livery to that shown in the previous view, though its condition was by now rather less pristine. The polished brass splasher beading adds a touch of style which was not perpetuated when the engine received its first 'proper' BR livery. Built in 1912, the engine moved north in April 1931, received a BR number in June 1948 and was eventually repainted in BR lined black. It was withdrawn in April 1954, by the end of which year, all the Scottish B12s had been withdrawn. Curiously there were still some fifteen Class D40 4-4-0s in stock at that time - below. (T.B.Owen - Ref: SC256)

June 1952 at Haymarket shed and under the grime Scottish 'Director', Class D11/2 No.62677 Edie Ochiltree, *is still carrying the post war LNER green livery albeit with BR trappings. The lettering is plain Gill Sans including the painted name, in the best Cowlairs North British tradition. Much of the livery detail is obscured and this is not helped by the angle of the sunlight in this view. Built by Kitson & Co. in September 1924 No.6384 (original LNER number) was painted green until demoted to lined black under the 1928 economies. Sixteen D11/2s received post war green and subsequently BR lined black, lining details of which can be seen on the tender in front of No.62677. By contrast, Gorton works (the 'home' of the design) painted none of the former GCR Class D11/1s in post-war green and several remained plain black until withdrawal.* (T.B.Owen - Ref: SC386)

Great North of Scotland Railway tender engines were exclusively 4-4-0s and used on both passenger and freight services. It is a measure of much of the GNSR system's restricted axle loading and the LNER's impecunity that forty 4-4-0 locomotives, of LNER Classes D40 and D41, were still around at Nationalisation. One of the later superheated D40s built in 1920 No.62278 Hatton Castle *stands on Kittybrewster shed, in ex-works condition, in September 1949. All eighteen members of the class taken over by BR eventually received lined black livery as shown here. No.62278 was renumbered into the BR series in January 1949. Note that the Inverurie type panel on the cabside does not follow the rear splasher contour; both number and tender lettering are set low down within their panels. The Route Availability RA3 is painted below the number. The axle loading of the D40s theoretically put them in the more restricted RA4 category, but they were permitted over a number of RA3 routes.* (J.M.Jarvis - Rcf: SC105)

The former GNSR works at Inverurie helped to maintain the NBR J36 0-6-0s and after the war two examples were painted green, though the locomotives, Nos. 5330 and 5211, were not allocated to the GNSR section. No.5330 received its green livery in October 1946 and was repainted green with BR markings and number in August 1948. It lasted in this condition, shown here at Dundee shed in 1949, until November 1951. Surprisingly Cowlairs did not paint any J36s green, thus none of the well known named examples were given the livery. Note how the flared section of the tender has been treated as a separate panel. No.65330 has a shed plate but as yet no smokebox door number plate. The photograph provides a particularly nice study in weathering, especially brake blocks and reversing rod, combined with the liberal dose of ash. The locomotive remained at Dundee until September 1960 and spent its final years before withdrawal, in June 1962, working out of Hawick shed. (J.Robertson - Ref: SC273)

Ex NBR 0-6-0 tank, LNER Class J83, No.68481 pauses outside its home depot of Haymarket in 1949. Waverley station required four pilot engines and so six J83s were repainted apple green at Cowlairs Nos.8472/3/4/7/8/81. No.8481 was given a BR prefix in May 1948 along with 'BRITISH RAILWAYS' in full on the tank side. Given the way the number was crammed onto the bunker it would perhaps have been more logical to retain it under the lettering on the tank side, in LNER fashion. The lining out has fairly generous black borders with rounded corners. The lined green wheels have weathered quickly, ignored by the cleaners. The Waverley pilots continued to received preferential treatment, being later turned out in BR lined black whilst their sister engines remained plain. Built by Sharp Stewart in 1901 No.68481 was withdrawn from Haymarket shed in February 1962. (J.Robertson - Ref: SC276)

ABOVE: *The experimental BR dark blue livery with LNWR style lining is displayed particularly well in this view of former GWR King Class 4-6-0 No.6025* King Henry III *at Chippenham in 1950. The tender displays the original full lettering (in this case in a non-standard sans-serif style) applied in April/May 1948 to Nos.6001/9/25/26. No.6025 was based at Plymouth Laira during 1948 to work the 'Cornish Riviera' service. Note that the cream and grey is applied to the upper edge only of the splashers, whilst the red line forms a panel. This red panel is repeated under the nameplate. As with other examples in this chapter, the engine is carrying the colour which some observers described as having a 'purple' hue.* (K.H.Leech - Ref: BRW332)

BELOW: *King Class 4-6-0 No.6009* King Charles II *stands at Chippenham with a stopping train in 1949. It was one of four Kings painted experimental blue in 1948. The tenders were initially lettered in full, in what was described as plain white (see previous view). By the last week in July 1948, No.6009's livery had been altered with the lion and wheel symbol illustrated here appearing on the tender.* King Charles II *was repainted standard blue early in 1950. Based at Old Oak Common, No.6009 spent the summer of 1948 working the 'Cornish Riviera' between Paddington and Plymouth, a service which carried experimental coach livery for one season only. In 1949 the stock appeared in red and cream. Built in March 1928, No.6009 was withdrawn along with the majority of its sisters in Autumn 1962, their fate sealed by the arrival of increasing numbers of 'Western' diesel hydraulics from Swindon and Crewe.* (Colour-Rail - Ref: BRW129)

OPPOSITE, ABOVE *The original GWR King Class 4-6-0 No.6000* King George V *displays BR standard blue livery as it stands at Chippenham with an up express in July 1949. It was only two weeks out of Swindon in this new livery; previously it had been green with 'BRITISH RAILWAYS' in full on the tender and the prefix W to the number. The class was the only GWR express passenger design to receive BR blue livery. The brass cases above the numberplate on the cabside contained bronze medals presented by the Baltimore & Ohio Railway; their positioning meant that the route restriction code, double red, was placed below the numberplate on this particular locomotive. The nameplate has the traditional black backing, though for a short period around early 1950 some engines received red backgrounds to their nameplates. Not all works applied a double white line to the cylin-*

Castle Class No.4085 Berkeley Castle *entered Swindon Works in August 1948 and as no clear livery directive had yet emerged from the Railway Executive it was painted in GWR livery with 'BRITISH RAILWAYS' in full on the tender in GWR style lettering; indeed, during this period many locomotives appear from Swindon with no 'branding' at all. By this time, however, most engines were receiving smokebox door numberplates with the inexplicable exception of the Castles. It was January 1949 before the final decision on the new colour schemes was made. In this 1949 scene at Chippenham, The 1925 vintage locomotive is attached to a much newer Hawksworth pattern tender; behind the Reading based engine is a concertina brake third. Both this and the succeeding vehicle appear still to be in pre-war livery.* (K.H.Leech - Ref: BRW334)

ABOVE: *Castle Class 4-6-0 No.4091* Dudley Castle *stands at Chippenham in 1949, probably on a running-in turn. In 1948 the engine had entered Swindon Works during May and reappeared in the experimental light green livery illustrated here. The lining out is red, cream and grey but the front buffer plank seems to have retained its GWR orange/red colour. The firebox was not lined out at all, a break with previous GWR practice that remained when the dark green livery with orange and black was readopted. Contemporary sources also report green-backed nameplates and cabside numberplates with this experimental livery, though in this view they seem black-backed. The non-standard smokebox door numberplate was reported to have been in brass, though it looks more like polished steel here. Note the small dark cream/yellow sans serif lettering on the tender. This is smaller than that used on other regions - closer in size and spacing to the GWR style 'BRITISH RAILWAYS' (see previous view). The allocation is still to be found just behind the bufferbeam on the angle iron, PDN (Paddington) actually signifying Old Oak Common, which shed worked a number of experimental liveried trains in 1948. No.4091, built in July 1925 was withdrawn from Old Oak Common in January 1959.* (K.H.Leech - Ref: BRW335)

ABOVE: *Shrewsbury based Star Class 4-6-0 No.4040* Queen Boadicea *starts away from Chippenham station with a stopping train in 1950. The livery, a typical Swindon hybrid of the period, is basically GWR green without ownership markings, except the BR style smokebox door numberplate. With new Castles still being turned out at Swindon until 1950 the Stars were coming towards the end of their careers and most succumbed to the torch in the early 1950s. No.4040, built in March 1911, was withdrawn in June 1951.* (K.H.Leech - Ref: BRW352)

OPPOSITE, ABOVE: *BR-built Merchant Navy Class 4-6-2 No.35024 is captured in April 1949 in an experimental shade of blue with red stripes in the Bulleid manner - happily one of the most short-lived livery variations of the early BR period! It was the last engine to appear in experimental blue and the only one to display the red stripes. It carried this livery between 12th February 1949 and 2nd March 1949; the lining was then amended to the new standard for express passenger engines: black and white. A hand painted BR lion and wheel symbol adorns the tender. Both numbers displayed, on the cabside and smokebox, are in Gill Sans figures. When it first appeared from Eastleigh Works in November 1948 it had been painted Malachite green and ran with Battle of Britain type tender No.3333 until the delivery of its own 6000 gallon variety shown here. The nameplate is covered; the engine was later named* East Asiatic Company. *The MN 4-6-2 Class was the only Southern design to qualify for the BR blue livery, it being regarded as 'principal' passenger, 6ft 2in wheels notwithstanding - see also captions to the LNER design Class A2 4-6-2s, featured above.* (The late S.C.Townroe - Ref: BRS306)

OPPOSITE, BELOW: *This next view shows* East Asiatic Company *again, now No.35024, in the standard blue livery with two stripes of white-black-white lining and the bottom of the casing and cylinders painted black, a far more elegant presentation. The naming ceremony took place on 5th May 1949, shortly after a visit to Eastleigh Works. The cabside numbers are rendered in the standard off white colour. No.35024 is leaving Waterloo with a special to Weymouth on 21st June 1949, conveying HRH The Princess Elizabeth and HRH The Duke of Edinburgh in Pullman car* Cecilia. *The locomotive displays a Bournemouth line headcode with Nine Elms duty No.SPL1. No.35024 was actually an Exmouth Junction based engine but may have been used for this special train as it was only just over a month out of shops and one of only a few members of the class carrying the new standard blue livery at the time. In due course, 27 out of the 30 engines became blue and curiously, it was also No.35024 which was the first to become BR green (June 1951). The leading coaches are Bulleid designs, a semi-open brake third is followed by a corridor composite.* (The late S.C.Townroe - Ref: BRS307)

OPPOSITE, ABOVE: *The 1948 locomotive exchanges saw many interesting workings and performances over much of the BR network. The Bulleid West Country pacifics were certainly at the forefront in the latter respect, thanks in part to the lively driving style adopted by the Southern Region crews. No.34006 Bude worked a number of the 'mixed traffic category' test runs, although the SR engines were considerably more powerful than their rivals. It is seen here at Aylesbury in June 1948 with the 8.25am Manchester-Marylebone service. The LNER dynamometer car behind the locomotive shows that this was an up test run on either the 9th or 11th June. Four tests were carried out between the 8th-11th June, following familiarisation runs the week before. The LMS tender was provided to allow No.34006 to pick up water en route. The livery is Southern Malachite with BR numbers in SR style lettering, shaded black on the cabside, green above the buffer plank. The tender is plain black with white lettering.* (H.N.James - Ref: BRE39)

OPPOSITE, BELOW: *Un-named Battle of Britain 4-6-2 No.34083 awaits departure from Victoria with the 'Golden Arrow' in April 1949. The train had been reinstated after the war in April 1946 and until the advent of the Britannias, Bulleid pacifics of both types provided the motive power. The decorative arrows, headboard and flags certainly suited the unrebuilt engines. No.34083 was built at Brighton in October 1948 and allocated to Stewarts Lane, Battersea. It displays Malachite green livery with BR number and lettering in the usual Southern style of the time. No.34083 was later named* 605 Squadron. *Note the Stewarts Lane duty number pasted on the headcode disc.* (J.M.Jarvis - Ref: BRS19).

Bulleid West Country 'light' pacific No.s21C116 Bodmin *stands on Eastleigh shed in Spring 1948 in Southern Malachite green livery, which it received new in December 1945, but which now has 'BRITISH RAILWAYS' in full on the tender in Southern 'sunshine' style lettering with 's' prefix to the number (added in March 1948). In July 1948* Bodmin *received its BR number 34016. It carries the full air-smoothed casing with medium length smoke deflectors. The bunker of a Class Z 0-8-0 tank (No.95?) also carries the 's' prefix to the number in Bulleid style green shaded characters. This suggests the picture was probably taken in March 1948, as shortly afterwards 30000 was added to the numbers of former Southern Railway locomotives, save for those to Bulleid's own design which all carried running numbers devised according to Bulleid's own preferred system. In the case of the pacifics, the MNs received numbers in the new 35xxx series and the light 4-6-2s went into the 34xxx number block.* (The late S.C.Townroe - Ref: BRS424)

Three Lord Nelson Class 4-6-0s acquired experimental apple green livery with red, cream and grey lining: Nos.30856/61/4. No.30856 Lord St. Vincent was repainted at Eastleigh in Spring 1948 and transferred to Bournemouth along with No.30861 Lord Anson in order to work the 7.20am Bournemouth West-Waterloo and the 3.30pm(SX) and 1.30pm(SO) Waterloo-Bournemouth return. These services were to be run with plum and spilt milk coaches allowing the public to judge the new liveries for an eight week period during the summer. The photograph was taken in August 1948 and is believed to be at Poole, approaching Holes Bay Junction. The locomotive is hauling the six-coach Weymouth portion of the down services mentioned above (Pendragon Collection - Ref BRS 872)

OPPOSITE, ABOVE: *This picture was taken at Eastleigh only three or four months after the earlier picture of* Bodmin *(above) but things have already moved on. Nearest the camera, West Country Pacific No.34022* Exmoor *is painted Malachite green combined with yellow letters edged in black - a type similar to the 'sunshine' style but probably unshaded. Next in line comes Battle of Britain Class No.34064* Fighter Command *in experimental light green with red, cream and grey lining. The green covers all the bodyside casing and cylinders, whereas No.34022 has the lower portions painted black. The lettering is a rather bold sans serif style. A Class Z 0-8-0 tank No.30956 follows, painted plain black with 'BRITISH RAILWAYS' in full using SR sunshine lettering. Last in line is the Royal T9 4-4-0 No.30119 in Malachite(?) green with black and white lining and 'BRITISH RAILWAYS' in full in sunshine lettering. Although said to be taken in July 1948 the shot is more likely to have been taken in early June.* (The late S.C.Townroe - Ref: BRS442)

OPPOSITE, BELOW: *West Country pacific No.34011* Tavistock *stands at Exmouth Junction shed in June 1949. The Plymouth Friary based engine is waiting for the return leg of duty No.613, the down 'Devon Belle' (Plymouth portion), having brought the up service to Exeter Central earlier in the day. No.34011 is finished in early BR experimental green (often described as apple green) with two bands of red, cream and grey lining. Note the red line is innermost at the top and bottom. In this view the engine has black paint around the cylinders, although it appears the rest of the engine and tender are still all green. The lettering appears to be a rather curious hybrid of unshaded sans serif in a bold 'sunshine' shape. When it first received this livery in the late spring of 1948 it still carried the circular 'Southern' plate on the smokebox, now replaced by a BR numberplate. Four light pacifics were repainted in this livery: Nos.34011/56/64/5.*

In December 1948, three new BB Class 4-6-2s, Nos.34086-8, appeared from Brighton Works in experimental green livery which differed from that shown in this and the previous view in that all three locomotives had a black band at the bottom of the casings on both engine and tender, similar to that of the Malachite green SR livery. Nos.43086-8 were allocated to Ramsgate shed to work experimental liveried services during Summer 1948. These comprised the 7.20am Ramsgate-Cannon Street and 5.15pm(SX) Cannon Street-Ramsgate (1.15pm SO), along with a Sunday only Ramsgate-Victoria working. (W.H.G.Boot - Ref: BRS164)

ABOVE: *This close up of Lord Nelson 4-6-0 No.30864* Sir Martin Frobisher *at Southampton Docks in July 1948, although rather washed out, does show details of the lining out applied to the experimental green LNs. Double red lines are applied to the boiler barrel and cylinders, with red cream and grey elsewhere. The lining on the cab is taken right over the top of the windows, whilst that on the tender is not carried onto the angled coal guard section at the top of the side sheet. The SR power classification A is placed below the number on the cabside as the lining prevents it from being displayed in the Southern fashion just behind the bufferbeam. The engine is carrying Royal Train headcode and both painted and metal surfaces are highly polished.* (The late S.C.Townroe - Ref: BRS367)

OPPOSITE, ABOVE: *Gently does it! The driver keeps a watchful eye on proceedings as N15 Class 4-6-0 No.30736* Excalibur is *turned at Bournemouth shed in 1949. This engine was the first of the LSWR N15s, built in 1918 to the design of Robert Urie. Maunsell perpetuated the design after Grouping with the King Arthur Class engines. The 'Arthurian' name series was created by the Southern Railway in the mid-1920s and included the pregroup Urie examples. After the war No.736 was painted in Malachite green with sunshine lettering in July 1947. From February 1949 the BR number was added in SR characters as seen here. It ran in this condition until repainted in BR green in November 1950 and remained in that livery until withdrawal six years later. Note the Lemaitre multiple blast pipe and large diameter chimney fitted in 1940.* (The late S.C.Townroe - Ref: BRS311)

OPPOSITE, ABOVE: *At Nine Elms shed in May 1950, LSWR King Arthur Class 4-6-0 No.30742* Camelot *appears to have had a period of inactivity judging by the rust on the wheels - many Southern locomotives spent periods in store particularly during the winter months. No.742 returned to Malachite green after the war in August 1946. The cab front apears to be black, though some sources suggest that green was used with this livery - possibly either, depending on where painted. When it received its BR number in October 1948 Malachite livery was retained, but with proper BR style Gill Sans insignia, albeit painted in yellow to match the lining. Note how the number and tender lettering have been applied at the same height above rail level. A front numberplate has been attached although shed plates did not appear on the Southern Region until shortly after this view was taken. BR lined green was finally applied in December 1951.* (T.B.Owen - Ref: BRS389)

RIGHT: *Drummond's Class T9 4-4-0s, built around the turn of the Century, were his most successful passenger design for the LSWR, a reputation further enhanced after rebuilding with superheaters from 1922 onwards. No.119 was one of the first batch, constructed at Nine Elms Works in 1899 and during Southern days was often used on Royal workings. In 1935 it was given special treatment with the smart Maunsell green livery embellished with gilt lettering and burnished pipework. In this condition it ran mostly on special and excursion trains in addition to its Royal duties. After the war the universal plain black once again gave way to green, this time Malachite with black and white lining. This was renewed in May 1948 as shown here with its BR number and lettering applied in Southern 'sunshine' style. The contemporary issue of* Railway Observer *noted the colour as light green and No.30119 is seen thus at Dorchester c.1950-1. Although officially 'Malachite', there is a blue cast to the green in this and other contemporary colour pictures of No.30119 at the time which suggest that there may have been some variation in the shade applied to this engine, though film degradation cannot be excluded. BR number and shedplates have now been fitted (shed plates were not fitted to SR locos until the summer of 1950) and the organ pipe whistle fitted in 1935 has disappeared. The decorative star on the smokebox may reflect the engine's Scottish ancestry; this type of embellishment was more often found north of the border. No.30119 was withdrawn in December 1952 still carrying its green livery. Note the black tops to the leading and coupling rod splashers.* (T.B.Owen - Ref: BRS484)

BELOW: *Class M7 0-4-4 tank No.30241 at Nine Elms shed in May 1952. The engine still sports Malachite green livery with black and yellow lining. Accepting the margin of error implicit in colour photography, this shade seems undoubtedly a different hue (though officially the same colour) as that shown on No.30119 in the previous picture. The characters are sans serif in yellow, matching the lining rather than the standard cream, though in this respect it should be mentioned that the BR insignia colour was not wholly standardised at this time, especially on the Southern Region; a number of shades, white, cream, off-white and even silver-white could be seen. Six M7s employed on station pilot and ECS duties at Waterloo were repainted Malachite green from December 1946 and three of them were repainted green in the early BR period, including No.30241 in July 1948. It did not loose its special finish until March 1953 when it received BR lined black. No.30241 was a long-lived engine: built in 1899, it was withdrawn from Eastleigh shed in July 1963.* (T.B.Owen - Ref: BRS552)

In 1946 the Southern Railway purchased fourteen 0-6-0 tanks built to a US Army Transportation Corps design. SR No.73 was built by Vulcan Iron Works, Wilkes-Barre, Pennsylvania, USA in 1943 as US Army No.1974. On their receipt, the SR modified various features including the regulator, bunker, cab windows and ventilator and the locomotives entered traffic in 1947. They were classified USA tanks by the Southern and put to work in Southampton docks. The livery shown here is a transitional one. The number has the prefix 's' to denote Southern Railway origin, 'BRITISH RAILWAYS' in full being applied in green-shaded SR style characters. Eventually renumbered BR No.30073 it remained in the Southampton area until withdrawal in December 1966. (Colour-Rail - Ref: BRS842)

LSWR Class 02 0-4-4 tanks became the mainstay of Isle of Wight services soon after the Southern took them over in 1923. This situation remained until the demise of steam in 1967, despite the age of the class. By the latter date the system was much reduced by closures in the 1950s and 1960s. In this view, No.32 Bonchurch, a 1928 import to the island, stands on Newport shed in May 1952. It had been repainted Malachite green in 1948 with BR in full on the tank sides. By the time this picture was taken a BR shed plate had also been fitted: 71E for Newport. None of the island's engines ever carried a smokebox door number-plate. No.32 was transferred to Ryde shed in November 1957 when Newport closed and was withdrawn in October 1964. Latterly the Isle of Wight engines were painted BR lined black. The nameplates had to be lowered in order to fit the lion and wheel symbol on the tank sides. (T.B.Owen - Ref: BRS566)

Ex-LBSCR Class E1 0-6-0T No.4 Wroxall *was another Southern import to the Isle of Wight. Numbered B131 by the Southern it arrived in the island in June 1923 and was renumbered into the IOW system. In this May 1949 view taken at Newport shed the livery is Malachite green with black and yellow lining. 'BRITISH RAILWAYS' has been applied in full in shaded yellow characters by patch painting out the 'Southern' branding - note the lighter strip of paint. This may have two explanations: either the variability of the Malachite or more likely, the way the colour darkened over time in service, despite the Island's reputation for keeping its locomotives clean. When No.4 was withdrawn from Ryde shed in October 1960 as the last of four E1s to work on the island, it gave the Class 02s a complete monopoly of IOW services until the end of steam.* (W.H.G.Boot - Ref: BRS115)